T0339114

WILDERNESS

Fly Fishing and Public Lands in the American West

OF HOPE

QUINN GROVER

University of Nebraska Press | Lincoln

© 2019 by Quinn Grover

Acknowledgments for the use of copyrighted
material appear on page xi, which constitutes
an extension of the copyright page.

Library of Congress
Cataloging-in-Publication Data
Names: Grover, Quinn, author.
Title: Wilderness of hope: fly fishing and public
lands in the American west / Quinn Grover.
Description: Lincoln: University of Nebraska
Press, [2019] | Series: Outdoor lives series |
Includes bibliographical references.
Identifiers: LCCN 2019005274
ISBN 9781496211804 (cloth: alk. paper)
ISBN 9781496217943 (epub)
ISBN 9781496217950 (mobi)
ISBN 9781496217967 (pdf)
Subjects: LCSH: Fly fishing—West
(U.S.)—Anecdotes. | Wilderness
areas—West (U.S.)—Anecdotes.
Classification: LCC SH456 .G74 2019 |
DDC 799.12/4—dc23 LC record available
at https://lccn.loc.gov/2019005274

Set in Scala OT by E. Cuddy.
Designed by L. Auten.

For TaNece, Paige, and Ella.

And for my father, who taught me to cast a
line and to love the places where lines are cast.

The rod and line,
True symbol of the foolishness of hope

WILLIAM WORDSWORTH, *The Prelude*

The wild requires that we learn the terrain, nod to all the plants and animals and birds, ford the streams and cross the ridges, and tell a good story when we get back home.

GARY SNYDER, *The Practice of the Wild*

CONTENTS

ACKNOWLEDGMENTS

Several chapters have been published previously—often in a slightly different form or under a different title. My thanks to the editors who worked with me and believed in my work enough to publish it.

An early version of "Five Days in the Wilderness" appeared in the now defunct *Fish Can't Read*.

"The Glimpse" and the first section of "Driving Conversations" (as "Premeditated Optimism") appeared in the *Flyfish Journal*.

"Funeral" appeared in the *Drake*.

"The Stump Ranch Fish" appeared in *Newfound*.

"Short Seasons" appeared in *Juxtaprose*.

"Kissing, Telling, and Invisible Trout" appeared in *Cirque*.

Various paragraphs and sections of some chapters started out as blog posts on my retired blog *In the Back Eddy* or the blog *Chi Wulff*, run by Dry Fly Media. My thanks to those who read and commented on those pieces.

A heartfelt thanks to those who read chapters (or the whole book) and gave me encouragement and advice, especially Leslie Ovard, Jaren Watson, Trent Olsen, Riley Hebdon, and Emily Merrick. Thanks to Rob Taylor (and everyone at University of Nebraska Press) for taking a chance on me. Thanks to Margaret Mattern, Haley Mendlik, and Sarah C. Smith for exemplary editing. Thanks to all the fishing partners over the years, especially Packer, my brothers, and my dad. Thanks to my mom, who showed me what it means to be a reader. And thanks to my wife and daughters for more than I can describe.

PROLOGUE

We simply need that wild country available to us,
even if we never do more than drive to its edge
and look in. For it can be a means of reassuring
ourselves of our sanity as creatures, a part of the
geography of hope.

WALLACE STEGNER, *The Sound of Mountain Water*

I caught my first fish using a fly rod on a Boy Scout outing. I was thirteen years old. We were camped along a small creek in central Utah, and I had insisted on taking my fly rod, even though I had yet to actually catch anything using it. The stream—just three or four feet wide in many places and bordered by bunches of willows—snaked through a meadow carpeted with the green grass of a wet summer.

I spotted the fish rising in a flat, unprotected section of river between willow bunches and I felt suddenly—alarmingly—visible. I decided to kneel before making the cast because the landscape was so wide open. I felt exposed—as a fisherman, as a beginner, as an outsider in a wild place. I'd like to believe that I sensed something divine in the presence of the rising of a trout, some sort of holiness, something that demanded reverence. But really, I was just scared I was going to screw up my one chance.

I hadn't really practiced casting from a kneeling position so I kind of crouched as low as I could and made my best attempt at a cast. I think my fly hit the grass behind me as it turned over. I was using a rod I had purchased at a local department store for twelve dollars, and I was a long way from the security of my backyard, where my father had taught me to cast a piece of yarn toward a bucket. I don't really remember the cast. I am sure it was poor and the fish rose out of extreme hunger or curiosity or perhaps pity.

I think the fly I was using was an Adams, but I really don't know. I am sure it had feathers because it was a dry fly. When I think about it now, I like to imagine that fly and that fish when I read Emily Dickinson's poem: "'Hope' is the thing with feathers—/ That perches in the soul" (1964, 34).

I am not the first fly angler to connect that poem to the act of fly fishing and the fly itself. Ted Leeson used Dickinson's poem as a starting point for a great essay about the idea that the fly is a physical manifestation of hope in his book *The Habit of Rivers*. But just because the connection is not particularly original doesn't mean it's any less powerful for me now, especially when I think about that day and that fish. Hope was all I had to go on. Hope and the belief that the fish's riseform (what fly anglers call the sound and sight of a fishing rising to eat a bug from the water's surface) was a part of what Dickinson called the "tune without words" (1964, 34), a song I desperately wished to hear then and still search for today.

The name of that little Utah stream was Sevenmile Creek. It runs through a high meadow before it is squeezed into a canyon, then dumps into Johnson Valley Reservoir at the canyon's mouth. When my scout troop pulled in to the meadow to set up camp along its banks, I remember gazing around in awe. The meadow and the pine trees showed a bit more greenery than is usual in the brown Intermountain West. It seemed like a place worth knowing. The entirety of Sevenmile Creek—from its headwaters to its terminus—is located on national forest land. It's a landscape open and available to you and me and some thirteen-year-old kid somewhere who just bought a cheap fly rod or maybe was given one by his grandfather. Thinking about hope as the thing with feathers and Emily Dickinson and my own past in that place is important to me because Sevenmile Creek and all the land that surrounds it are part the geography of my life. For me, they help to form what Wallace Stegner, a novelist and historian of the American West, called "the geography of hope."

The phrase "geography of hope" comes from Stegner's famous Wilderness Letter, a document written in 1960 and addressed to government researchers gathering public comments for a report on the value of wilderness—a report that was part of the debate surrounding what eventually became the Wilderness Act. The letter has since become an open letter, a manifesto for all to see. Stegner published the letter in his book *The Sound of Mountain Water*, and today, when I searched for it online, I found it on the websites for The Wilderness Society and the University of Montana's Wilderness Connect program, among other places. I have encountered the letter and passages from it in material from the Sierra Club and other conservation organizations. A year or so ago, the *Whitefish Review* in Montana published an entire issue dedicated to the idea of the geography of hope.

What strikes me most about the phrase "geography of hope"— and perhaps what has made it so enduring—is its beautiful ambiguity. What does "geography" mean in this context? A nation? A watershed? A bioregion? A landscape? The fact that this term is difficult to pin down is part of its power. We stretch that geography far enough to cover what we need it to cover. For me, it tends to border trout streams. For Stegner, it seems to cover everything west of Nebraska but especially those places where humanity's mark remains invisible or easy to ignore.

Stegner's use of the phrase—as well as the context of the Wilderness Letter itself—suggest that at least a portion of the geography of hope should be protected from humanity's reach. He hopes to save something within the geography that might otherwise be lost. He argues that this "wild country" should be preserved somehow and contends that preservation is valuable for all of humanity, even those who don't hike or fish or wander through protected areas. Such country, argues Stegner, is important "even if we never do more than drive to its edge and look in" (1997, 153). But we are left to wonder a bit as readers just what we might be looking at. How does a geography of hope appear to the viewer? I suppose it depends on who is doing the looking. Different people see different things—a concept that is important and hopeful all on its own.

Conservation organizations have seen the geography of hope as a signifier for protecting parcels of public land from development. The majority of public land in the United States is located between the Pacific Coast and the western portions of the Great Plains. According to a recent report by the Congressional Research Service, the federal government owns 46.4 percent of the land in eleven western states and a mere 4 percent of the lands in the other states that make up the lower forty-eight (Vincent, Hanson, and Argueta 2017). Because so much public land is concentrated in the West, Stegner's "hope" is tinged with American popular culture's obsession with the American West as a land of hope. This obsession predates Stegner and is perhaps most prevalent in the nineteenth century. "Eastward I go by force," wrote Henry David Thoreau in 1862, "but Westward I go free" (2001, 234). Stegner himself often refers to the American West as a region of hope. In 1992 he wrote that "the West at large is hope's native home . . . magnificently endowed and with the chance to become something unprecedented and unmatched in the world" (1992, xv). From colonial times, Americans of European descent have measured themselves against the wilderness as both a metaphor and a reality; they have established communities in it, chopped it down, pushed it back, and lived with the land sometimes pushing them back, all the while using reams of paper to write about what wilderness means. The wilderness they wrote about was primarily located geographically to the west and often represented a myriad of possibility, even if those possibilities were sometimes mere fantasies.

For the conservation movement, then, the West represents an opportunity to protect wild lands—those geographies of hope—from development, from destruction, often from becoming another version of what they see in the nation's East. So hope comes to mean more than simply the West as a region but a kind of unspoiled West, a chance to keep from making the mistakes of the past, an opportunity to preserve rather than destroy.

But the hope of the West cuts both ways. Most of the nineteenth-century hope that brought settlers west was material in nature. Easterners came west not merely to "look in," as Stegner puts it, but to dig in and extract wealth. For many, this extractive definition of hope still lives, and those who use it look longingly, even hopefully at the public lands of the American West. In this way, those arguing for the sale or development or even the loosening of regulations of public lands might argue that they are also seeing these landscapes as geographies of hope that an eastern government is keeping out of their reach. I don't find myself convinced by this argument, but I do feel like I understand it. Those who hold this position feel they are being denied something they see as fundamentally American: the opportunity to use the land for monetary gain. Such hope is, I think, easily justified by our economic and environmental past.

My own feelings about the geography of hope don't conform exactly to either of these definitions. For me, what makes public lands special and important, the value in which their hope resides, is that they can provide something for the public and for the landscape at large—a kind of wealth for all of us, not just economic wealth for the privileged few. That something may not be financial, but it is available to anyone who can manage to find it—a connection with the landscape that is guttural and immediate, a connection that cannot be described in monetary terms, a relationship with our ecological counterparts that is equal and important, that restores "our sanity as creatures"—to use Stegner's language—in ways we must work hard to even understand.

Because so much of America's public lands are located in the Intermountain West, this region is where arguments about the use and limits of those lands rage the loudest. At their core these arguments are about the meaning of hope and just what a geography of hope might look like. For some, such a geography should be free in that it lacks regulation and limits. It should be free and available to develop and purchase and mine and graze. For others, it should be free from roads and people and even the signs that people might exist. For still others—such as the indigenous groups that banded together to help establish Bears Ears National Monument in Utah—a geography of hope links to a past that extends well beyond a mere century or two, a connection with landscape forged over millennia that is entangled in culture, history, and ancestry in ways that many Americans can't really imagine. Stegner's ambiguity means that geographies of hope are moving targets, changing based on who is making the arguments and how they might define the slippery, beautiful, tension-filled ideas of landscape, geography, identity, and hope.

The essays in this book are about what those western landscapes—those geographies of hope—mean to me. I grew up in the Salt Lake Valley of Utah. I don't remember how old I was when I first went fishing with my father, but I am certain that the trip took us to a fishery located on public lands. My father taught me to fish—first with spinning gear and eventually with a fly rod—and fly fishing has become an integral part of who I imagine myself to be. Since that day on Sevenmile Creek, fly fisherman has been a central part of my identity, along with the roles father, son, husband, and citizen. I wrote the initial drafts of most of these essays between 2010 and 2014. At the time I was working as a technical writer in Idaho Falls. I was making a modest salary and fishing when I wasn't working, attending church, coaching my daughters' soccer teams, and taking my wife out to dinner. In other words, my life was one version of what many people think of (for better or worse) as distinctly American. I live in a small western suburban town with a middle-class income and middle-class lifestyle. Certainly, America is altogether too complex and varied for any one person's experiences to stand in as the American experience, so my life is one kind of American experience but not a particularly unique kind of experience in many ways.

I began writing this book because I wanted to figure out why—with all these other interests competing for my time—I felt the need to venture out through desert vistas and up mountain canyons to wild waterways filled with trout. Why was I drawn to these places? What was I looking for, and did I even know it when I found it? Somewhere along the way I began to realize that one of the most American things about my American experience was that it took place primarily on public lands and in public waters. While I searched for the "why" of my identity as a fly fisherman, I instead stumbled on the "how" of that identity: I was a fly fisherman—at least in part—because public lands and access to the great trout waters of the West made such an existence possible. I was a fly fisherman because Sevenmile Creek ran through the middle of Fishlake National Forest, a place where a thirteen-year-old kid with a fly rod could kneel and cast a "thing with feathers" at a rising trout.

From the time I began this project to the present, the battle over public lands has intensified. And it has become clear to me as I have edited and shaped these essays that these stories serve as my own argument about the importance of wildness and the role of public lands. Some of these stories take place on water in wilderness areas that were established through the Wilderness Act, the very legislation that Stegner wrote his letter for. Other stories take place in national parks, state parks, national forests, and land owned by the Bureau of Land Management. Nearly all of these stories take place in rivers where laws ensure public access to streams—laws that are currently under attack in many western states, including my home state of Utah. This book isn't an explicit argument about what we should do with any one parcel of public land or any one section of a public waterway. Instead, it is an attempt to document the connection to place that public lands make possible. Therefore, these essays don't dive into the political firestorms raging around places like Bears Ears National Monument. Instead, I have attempted to describe— when applicable—the role that specific public lands have played in my own connection to the landscapes and waters of the West.

I hope these essays convey the fact that I have done more than simply drive to the edge and look in. I have laced up boots and shouldered packs and hiked trails into wilderness looking for wildness, searching for trout. I have pushed boats of various sizes and shapes into the West's lakes. And most of all I have waded into the region's clear, cold, clean rivers, felt their geologic pull against my knees and shins, casting a fly with, as Norman Maclean puts it, "the hope that a fish will rise" (2001, 104). My experiences in these places are not particularly unique, and per- haps this is why I think they are important. I have not quit my job to go fishing or taken a year off to hike the Pacific Crest Trail. I am still a middle-class guy living a middle-class life. I haven't dedicated my life entirely to spending time in the public lands of the West, but I can't imagine my life without those lands. If my experience describes anything important, I hope that it provides a case study in just how integral such landscapes and waterways can be to all westerners—all Americans—not just those with the loudest voices in the public lands' shouting match or those who live in the counties that border public lands.

There is a tendency in arguments about public lands to charac- terize those involved in the debate at the extremes: rural ranchers who hate the government and covet the landscape; East Coast or California elites who donate to the Sierra Club but wouldn't recognize the West outside of Yosemite, Yellowstone, or Vail, Colorado; energy and mining companies who would suck the fossil fuels and minerals out of the ground and leave desolation in their wake; environmental terrorists who care more about trees than people. But these caricatures fail to capture the complexity of real people, and they render large segments of the western U.S. populace invisible. Think of those people who might go backpacking on the weekends and to work on Monday morning, those people who worry about the future and the present of the region for all kinds of different reasons. I'd like to think this book provides one such voice that defies the caricatures of the debate, though I don't claim it to be the essential voice by any stretch.

Besides the Wilderness Letter, the idea Wallace Stegner is perhaps most famous for is his view that the attribute that most separates the American West from the American East is a lack of water. The arid West regards water as a scarce resource, while the humid East is primarily worried about too much water rather than not enough. For Stegner, this distinction is fundamental because it permeates the cultures of the two regions and helped to create the mythology of the American West: "Aridity makes all the difference," he writes. "Aridity inspired barbed wire and the windmill, altered laws and social organization, profoundly affected men, myths, and moralities" (1992, xii).

This book is also about the water of the West, that most precious western resource. The laws and social organizations Stegner references have historically been altered and formed as a means of growing western cities and protecting western farmers and ranchers, groups whose primary water sources have been western rivers. But as the West changes, more and more westerners are making their living from recreation along and in the waterways of the West by doing something other than farming or ranching. This means that the battles over public lands are being fought concurrently with battles over public waterways.

Most of this book is about fly fishing. There are places where the language waxes technical, slipping into the Latin names of insect and trout species and listing the various sizes and shapes of trout flies that anglers use to imitate those insects and catch those trout. For me, such details are indistinguishable from the landscapes and waterways themselves. My connection to the trout streams of the West is steeped in the residents of those streams—the bugs and fish that inhabit western rivers and lakes—and the language that helps me understand those residents.

In the mid-1990s, environmental historian William Cronon published an essay titled "The Trouble with Wilderness: Or, Getting Back to the Wrong Nature." In the essay, Cronon argues that America's relationship with wilderness is founded on two complimentary concepts: the idea that the wilderness is a place to flee from civilization in order to find God and the idea that taming the frontier is fundamental to American character. These two ideas work together to reinforce the larger idea that wilderness—and, by extension, nature—are necessarily separate from civilization and humanity. So when Thoreau goes to Walden Pond or John Muir goes to the Sierras, they are escaping from civilization into nature. One of the troubles with this dualistic view is that it implies that the best way to save nature is to remove humanity from it altogether. Cronon argues that this idea leads us to think that saving a parcel of wilderness far from our homes gives us license to treat the "civilized" landscapes we do inhabit as somehow unnatural and therefore beyond saving. We convince ourselves that wilderness areas in the far-off Wind River Range of Wyoming will make up for the fact that our cities might be damaging the environment nearby. A key to this self-deception is the idea that humans and nature are not one and same, as if nature is some kind of unknowable other and humans are not part of the natural world.

If this sounds familiar, it is probably because this view is prevalent in Stegner's Wilderness Letter. The idea that wild country needs saving even if all we do is "drive to its edge and look in" reinforces "the trouble" Cronon sees with America's historical conception of wilderness. But Stegner also notes that such places "can be a means of reassuring ourselves of our sanity *as creatures*" (1997, 153, emphasis added). This line is easy to skip over, but I think Stegner is fighting his own urge to see wilderness as separate and apart from humanity. To lose "our sanity as creatures" would be to forget that wilderness is by all rights our ancestral home, that we are wild creatures and that we cannot escape that wildness temporarily, only to return to it later when civilization wears us down. When read with Cronon's ideas in mind, Stegner's letter is ambivalent about this idea. It seems to want wilderness both as a part of humanity and as a retreat from humanity. In that way, it is not unlike the debate surrounding public lands. One side of the debate is characterized as wanting to lock up all public lands for good, restricting all access and leaving locals out in the cold. The other side is characterized as wanting to destroy all public lands for its own personal wealth. Stegner's internal conflict about the meaning of wilderness mirrors the public conflict about the meaning of public lands.

The idea that humanity and nature are fundamentally separate is so present in our conception of nature that it can be difficult to detect and even harder to extract. I didn't encounter Cronon's essay until after I had written drafts of most of these essays. It didn't take me long to realize that my own identity as an angler was as ambivalent as Stegner's letter. I wanted to fish to both escape my office job and to remind myself that the office can be just as wild as a trout stream, that the same evolutionary forces are at play in both places. Perhaps this is because fly fishing lends itself to escape—it is generally practiced in beautiful, quiet landscapes far from other people—and because it forces one to approach that landscape on its own terms.

As a way of experiencing a landscape, fly fishing for trout is inherently active. An angler is required to observe the way a stream interacts with the surrounding topography and imagine where within a river's geography a trout might be feeding. When done well, fly fishing for trout requires a knowledge of aquatic entomology and an understanding of the feeding and predatory behavior of trout. Above all it requires an angler to participate in a natural world, to become a part of it in a way that is not merely observation. This participation must occur in accordance with the rules that nature itself has created. Fly fishing is not about taming nature but about understanding it and becoming a participant in it. The naturalist Aldo Leopold argues that a land ethic requires humanity to "think like a mountain" (1989, 129). Fly fishing asks its participants to think like a fish, which in turn requires a lot of thinking about rivers and water and bugs and ecosystems.

While many people describe fly fishing as an escape from civilization, it can also be a way of recalibrating one's own life. Trout, it is said, are interested in spending the least amount of energy to obtain the highest number of calories. While such a capitalistic metaphor might seem perverse or profane when applied to a native cutthroat trout, it illuminates the similarities between the office building and the river; it reveals that people and trout have a lot in common and describes one way that human nature and nature are inseparable. It reminds us that "wildness . . . dwells everywhere within and around us" (Cronon 1996, 25).

To that end, consider these essays not only as tales of an angler escaping back to wildness but as a series of stories about trying—and not always succeeding—to find a home in nature, a way of dwelling. For me, dwelling within nature should be the primary goal of our public lands management. We can't only see public lands as a series of landscapes from which we bar humanity's presence. Nor can we see them merely as extractive resources that we use to create wealth for a few and then throw away or build a city over. Rather, public lands must serve as a bridge between the human and nonhuman. We can use public lands as wildlife corridors that allow flora and fauna to migrate and connect with other bioregions while also connecting humans to other species. This view imagines public lands as bridges between bioregions rather than islands of wilderness in a sea of civilization. The fly-fishing industry is not perfect, but it does provide one small example of making a sustainable living and a meaningful life in the wild country of the American West; it finds a middle ground between our historical conceptions of wilderness and civilization. Writing about the idea of making a home in nature, another environmental historian—Dan Flores— suggests that we have to do more than just know the science or the history of the place. We have to get out and *feel* the places we want to call home: "Knowledge is insufficient in itself to enable humans to open to a place as home. Knowledge is too cerebral. Experiential, sensuous immersion—the way we've always done it—is the path home" (1999, 176). Fly fishing is my preferred method of "sensuous immersion"; it engages the senses and the mind in a way that I find intoxicating.

This book is my attempt to locate my own views of nature within the diverse views found in my culture, my own wildness with the wilderness. It is, as Cronon proposes, my practice of "remembrance and gratitude, for thanksgiving is the simplest and most basic of ways for us to recollect the nature, the culture, and the history that have come together to make the world as we know it" (1996, 25). To that end, I have organized the book into three sections, based on three themes I find in Stegner's ideas about wilderness. The first section is focused on the idea of reassurance. These essays are about how fly fishing and wild places have helped me to find a sense of belonging within nature. The second section includes essays focused on the act of reflection. Stegner argued that wild places allow humans to "look as deeply into themselves as anywhere I know" (1969, 153). Each essay in this section represents an attempt to do just that. The third section focuses on the idea of renewal. While I am cognizant of Cronon's warnings about the separation of wilderness and civilization, I also think trout streams and mountain lakes, places that have some measure of what I think of as explicit wildness, provide me with something that I can't get elsewhere. This section is an attempt to figure out what that something is. Taken together, these three ideas—reassurance, reflection, and renewal—make up some part of the unquantifiable reward that public lands can offer us. My memories of these places are my argument for protecting public lands from those that would make them less than public or less than ecologically healthy.

I don't remember all the details of my first fly-rod fish, not nearly as many as I would like. But those details seem less important when I think of what I do remember.

What I remember most is the take—that moment when the small trout rose up and took possession of the fly. Even now my mind plays back the evening light touching the water and the circular rise of a small fish near the clay cutbank of a meadow creek. The rise was larger than the tiny rises the fish had been performing previously, which were likely efforts to eat miniscule midges. The thing with feathers was a substantial meal for a small meadow creek trout. I remember the green grass glistening on the opposite bank from what must have been an afternoon rain.

Ted Leeson writes eloquently about the moment when a trout rises to a dry fly. He captures why such instances are important, why we carry them with us, why we continue to search for them. He argues that the surface of a trout stream is a doorway to another world, a floating fly the door's key: "At the instant of the take, the boundary of surface is shattered. Hidden things are disclosed. . . . The take is the visual analog of an unanswered question, a curiosity satisfied, the visible confirmation that we have, if only locally and temporarily, understood some small thing about a river" (1994, 157). I remember the sudden feeling of connection between myself and that small cutthroat trout; I immediately felt tethered to the fish, to the river, to the green meadow valley and the forest as a whole in a way I hadn't been before. The take—that riseform, that connection—was like a spike in my veins, a symbol carved into my brain. It was an electric indication of life beneath the surface, the unforgettable sensation of being tied to a live wire trout and a landscape that did not offer itself up without some effort from me.

Something in that moment—the take and that electric pulse on the other end of the line—keeps pulling me back to water and to the public lands that allow me to access that water. Even now, each time I cast, I'm trying again to catch that first fish, that pan-sized cutthroat. I'm always trying, casting the thing with feathers. On a good day, I even succeed.

WILDERNESS OF HOPE

PART ONE

REASSURANCE

FRIDAYS

Somewhere between the jobless troutbum and the world-traveling fly-fishing gentleman, between wildness and civilization, between gray cities and green mountains, between the fly-fishing lodge and the hobo camp, you will find the working-class fly angler. He or she is not revered in angling literature nor lusted after by high-end lodges. He sees too little of trout streams and too much of paint-covered dry walls and bumper-sniffing traffic. For her, the waters of New Zealand and Argentina are fantastic dreams, like moon colonies or rivers filled with mermaids. The working-class angler is hidden in the currents of fly-fishing culture like a reliable, relatively colorless, twelve-inch rainbow, big enough to bend the rod but not worth hollering upstream to your fishing partner about.

For a time in college, I was more troutbum than student. It took me six years to eke out a bachelor's degree. Six years of mornings, evenings, and afternoons among the pocket water and aspen trees of the local rivers. I skipped class to go fly fishing. I took a semester off to go fly fishing. I took out another student loan, and I went fly fishing. Eventually I graduated, my responsibilities multiplied, and my time standing in moving water among the wild places where trout live dwindled. I took a soul-crushing, river-damming, life-changing, bean-counting, blue-sky-intolerant, nine-to-five day job. If you consider life as a troutbum some sort of political movement, then I sold out.

It didn't happen all at once. At first I still made it out to the river almost every weekend and, if I was lucky, one or two evenings each week. My wife and I were living in Oregon, and a local river filled with hatchery trout—the working-class angler's meat and potatoes—served as an evening getaway. I would arrive an hour or two before dark and cast to rising hatchery trout. One night a run of salmon was in my favorite pool. Those rocket fish were launching themselves into the air to dislodge sea lice or entice a mate or satisfy some primal instinct. I didn't know why and I still don't, but I reeled in and climbed up onto a rock ledge to watch the show.

On the weekends we drove over the Cascades onto the high desert plateau of central Oregon. Among the cedar pines and sage, we fished the Metolius or the Deschutes or a fork of the Willamette River. My wife was introduced to salmonflies on the banks of the Deschutes. She learned quickly that those two-inch long, pterodactyl-like bugs were poor flyers and that any human was considered a nice airport terminal for insect layover and refueling. She decided to wait in the car. With the massive bugs all over me and the water, I caught one small fish on an even smaller mayfly nymph.

Eventually we moved to Idaho, where famous trout rivers beckoned. We had two daughters, and my job began to expand. I am a salaried worker, which means I work my share of evenings and weekends. In the heart of the Idaho winter, I arrive at work in the predawn dark and park my middle-class Toyota Camry among other such vehicles. I duck-walk across the icy parking lot under the sulfur-orange glow of towering street lamps. In the center of my personal office, a small four-sided column with a gray breaker box on the side that faces my desk rises from the floor to the ceiling, making half of the room difficult to access and creating a sense that the walls are somehow multiplying. The fluorescent lights flicker on when I flip the switch. The breaker box on the column is locked, and no one knows who has a key. Somewhere deep in the heart of the building there is an incessant, inhuman humming—like a mechanical heartbeat that has no need for rhythm. This humming never stops. It is accented by the tippy tapping of keystrokes, the whirring of computer fans, the bass-drum contracting and expanding of giant metal ducts hidden in the ceiling, the buzzing of cell phones, the voices of office banter, the low whisper of office gossip, the breathy exhale of office sighing, and the occasional ceramic clink of a mug against a glass coffeepot.

Like a synthesizer band from the 1980s, these sounds seem somehow unnatural to my ears. In large doses and over long periods unchecked, they make me feel like I imagine an android or a computer simulation might feel; they make me feel mechanical and constructed, like some kind of carbon-based machine. Every forty-five minutes government-issued software on my computer forces me to take a break, to protect my joints and muscles from my own efficiency. At such moments I cannot help but feel that I am a human component in a machine that would somehow work seamlessly if I were less human, less prone to muscle injuries and ligament damage brought on by what the workplace scientists call "repetitive stress." We office types injure ourselves not through sheer physical exertion but by repeating the same minor muscle movement hundreds of thousands of times without diversity. Such monotony is alien to our humanity. Our bodies— the delicate miracles that they are—flourish when we vary the muscle movements and the intensity. Humans evolved to meet the demands of working for and against the earth from sunrise to dark. Hunting and gathering required strength and stamina and courage in the face of a mastodon or the quickness to catch and cook and eat some ancestor of the jackrabbit. Now we are felled by a half-million mouse clicks.

None of this is to say that I long for those days as a college-kid troutbum or that I hate my job. Sure, I wish I could fish more. But I also wish I could spend more time with my children, more time writing, more nights eating quiet dinners with my wife, more time with my parents and my brothers and sister, with my nieces and nephews, watching sports or reading insightful books. I wish I had more time for all these things and perhaps that not as much of my time had to be spent putting myself at risk for repetitive stress injuries. But my job itself is challenging if cliché. I get to work with words, which I enjoy, and I get to work with scientists and engineers doing pretty incredible things, which is exciting. I wouldn't want to sacrifice all this or even most of it to chase the life of a fly-fishing guide. I love my family and my house and my retirement account too much for that. Besides, I am not convinced that a life spent repeatedly fishing the same river with high-dollar fly-fishing clients would feel any less mechanical.

One day I was browsing the tippet wall of my local fly shop when I heard the shop owner and one of his employees—a younger guy who doubled as a guide for a local outfitter—talking about steelhead fishing, about how hard it is and how much it means to catch each fish.

I was shopping for a new spool of 3x and maybe a leader, some fly-tying materials, and other odds and ends for an upcoming trip. I was eavesdropping because, well, that's an interesting conversation. The kind of conversation you only happen upon in a good fly shop. And I knew both participants, at least a little. The owner was an excellent guy with a generous streak who had helped me out a few times on my first fly-rod build, and the young kid knew a lot about fly tying and catching big trout on things like mouse patterns. I had picked his brain about such things enough times that he at least knew my face when I entered the shop.

I was hunched over and reaching for a spool, but I stopped short when I heard the kid say this:

"Maybe it's because I guide . . . but I tell you, the South Fork? That river holds no romance for me at all."

They were talking about a recent steelhead trip and the differences between fishing for chrome and fishing for trout. I stood up, eyeball to eyeball with several spools of 1x fluorocarbon. The

South Fork is the South Fork of the Snake, the most popular trout river among the locals in my town and a serious big-name river that people travel to from all over the country.

That idea, no romance, sounded familiar to me. It reminded me of that four-sided column in the middle of my office at work. This kid valued romance, or at least he felt that romance was missing, which seemed like a problem to him. Or maybe he knew something was missing, and romance was the only name he could put on it, some general word that describes the reason he started fishing in the first place, the reason many of us start fishing. The reason we still pull the waders on, the reason we travel to far-off rivers or dream about trout streams during boring staff meetings (and even not-so-boring staff meetings). I think that is what he missed—that spark that gets us out of bed for a day on the water. And romance was the best name he could give such a valuable, nameless thing.

Some listeners might have scoffed at such a sentiment. *Romance?* they might have said. *The South Fork has some big fish, hombre. Who cares about romance?* Well, maybe they wouldn't have used the word "hombre," but they might have said something to the effect that romance wasn't really a consideration when big fish and lots of them were involved. And that would have been a valid counterargument for a lot of anglers, I suppose. Such an argument could sway me, given the right circumstances.

But the shop owner didn't take that position. Rather, he said this: "I know exactly what you mean."

It was a simple phrase, the kind uttered four or five times a day by most of us without much thought. But I didn't get the impression that the owner was just being agreeable. I think he thought about it and answered that way because he did know exactly what the kid meant.

What the kid seemed to be saying, and what the shop owner seemed to be agreeing to, was the fact that guiding day in and day out on the same water, floating the same stretches and casting to the same banks, using the same flies and pulling fish out of all the same holes, could get mechanical. Performing any task ad nauseam feels mechanical, be it launching a drift boat or casting an indicator nymph rig or clicking your mouse a half-trillion times. This kid wasn't exactly clamoring for more trips down the South Fork on his day off. In fact, he was suggesting that fishing for trout on the South Fork wasn't nearly as much fun as it used to be.

I have taken just a few guided trips in my life. As a working-class angler, such trips are generally above my pay grade. The first guided trip I took was a walk-and-wade trip on the Madison River with a guide from Blue Ribbon Flies, Craig Matthews's shop in West Yellowstone, Montana. It was me and my father and brother. The guide was an interesting fellow who had started guiding on the San Juan River in New Mexico. He ended up in Montana during a road trip with his wife. They stopped at Raynolds Pass Bridge. He got out, rigged up, and walked down to the river. Within a dozen casts, he hooked and landed a fish (guides are pretty good at that sort of thing).

As he told it, he had the fish in the net when his wife walked down to the river and found him gazing at the trout in open wonder, a confused look on his face.

"Honey, this fish has teeth." He gaped. "Actual teeth."

I can see him pointing to the jaws of a Madison rainbow, his mouth ajar.

He then looked at his wife and said, "We're moving to Montana."

I told you he was interesting.

In truth, the stories he told that day were better than the fishing, which—through no fault of our entertaining and highly skilled guide—was exceptionally slow. It was August, in the middle of a hot streak that had lasted two months. The water was low, and the caddis had ended their evening madness nearly a month early in protest of extreme water temperatures and poor working conditions. The trout seemed glued to the bottom, except for a few browns that took hopper patterns out of boredom. Even the whitefish were tough to catch. So we were paying good money to not catch fish, something we had learned to do perfectly well on our own for free.

The guide talked about moving to Montana and spending two weeks floating the Madison from Raynolds Pass down to Ennis Lake so he could learn the river, sleeping on river islands and fishing every square inch of the fifty-mile riffle. He talked about guiding big wigs from Washington DC and messing with the Secret Service guys, about his minor league baseball career, about tying flies all winter so that he had enough to give away to schmoes like us whose boxes didn't contain a whole lot of anything that worked. On the surface, his life sounded down-right . . . romantic.

And maybe for him it was perfect. He was a great guide and a cool guy to spend a day with. But the more I thought about it the less convinced I became. He spent nine hours with us working hard and watching us catch a few meager fish in water he might have cleaned up in. He hadn't had a day off in nearly a month. He guided the first several years of his career on a river where the fish apparently didn't even have teeth. Once you got past all the great stories, it sounded just as mechanical as my own life. Wildness in life comes not simply from being away from buildings and streets and people; it comes from an ever-changing routine, from the unpredictability of wild places. Running the same float day after day and watching clients miss fish in all the same holes does not sound wild to me. I already hate untangling knots that are the products of my own tailing loop—I really don't want to untangle someone else's rat's nest. In short, I could understand how a guide could say that one of the great trout rivers in the West had lost all its romance. It only confirmed to me that I had made the right choice by not undertaking the guiding life.

I think it would chew me up, spit me out, and probably make me a steelhead fisherman.

The English have a saying: "You've lost the plot." It means you've lost track of purpose or sense, lost hold of the reins that keep you moving along the road of life, gone a little nuts. It is an idiomatic description just short of (or perhaps related to) losing your mind. I may have come close to losing the plot due to the mechanical nature of my life, if not for one fortunate turn of luck: the nine-eighty work week. I don't think the term "nine-eighty" is a common part of the American vernacular, so let me put it another way. My soul-crushing nine-to-five gives me every other Friday off.

I know it doesn't sound like a big victory, but there are weeks and months when that extra day is a key part of my survival. My wife, in her infinite compassion, has generally agreed that I should spend my one day every two weeks how I would like. So twice a month (sometimes three times—thank heavens for five-Friday months) I leave early Friday morning (or even better, late Thursday night) with my vehicle pointed toward some far-off national forest or state park and trout-filled water that can be fished comfortably in a day.

This intervention (along with the more robust occasional week-long adventure) is enough to break up the mechanical nature of modernity, at least for me. I escape the constant whirring of the corporate machine and reconnect—if only for a moment—with something that humanity has tried to hide from in air-conditioned office buildings. I don't need more than that regular reconnection, not right now anyway. I know that for some, the search for isolated wildness must take place more than one day every two weeks. These souls move to remote parts of Alaska or spend the entire summer backpacking in Wyoming. They head to Nepal or Patagonia and look for the wild earth as it was before modern man touched it and turned it into a fly wheel in the machine of progress. They seek danger and immersion, the heart of darkness or the light of true understanding—not the tourist wildness I encounter every other Friday in places I can drive to.

I don't take offense at the idea that my own occasional forays into places where trout live are merely a poseur's attempts to understand the things we have sacrificed in the name of progress, technology, and convenience. I also take no offense when people see no point in leaving their gray cities except to go to the ocean and lay on the beach. I am not in the business of one-size-fits-all behavior. Right now, in my life, these biweekly forays to trout country serve me well enough that the rest of my life is kept in balance. My children are happy, and one day I might be able to afford to send them to college. These things matter. I agree with those who argue that we need to stop thinking of a wilderness as someplace that can only exist without people and starting seeing our own existence as taking place *within* nature rather than in opposition to it. Cities themselves are a form of wildness; it's just that most of the animals in such wild places are humans rather than trout. A routine that puts me in a trout river one day every other week helps me remember that the fish and I are both residents of the same planet, that going fishing doesn't mean escaping from the world but visiting a portion of it that exists outside of a column-laden office and the hive-like machinery of an office-based existence.

Still, as a fisherman, when I read John Gierach's early work, I often react enviously to his tales of setting up camp and spending two weeks (or more) on the Henry's Fork or the Frying Pan or the South Platte. With two weeks of fishing time, the balance of power shifts a bit toward the fisherman. Suddenly a windy or rainy day is just a hiccup. And if the bugs aren't showing today, they are likely to be in the air and on the water in a day or two. Time is on the troutbum's side. The plight of the working-class fisherman is the opposite. It renders time especially scarce, which increases one's anxiety when spending it.

A good day trip is bound by location. If I am tripping solo (which I usually am), I try to keep the one-way drive time down to two and a half hours. I can hardly stand to be alone with myself in the car more for more than five hours in one day. I tire of hearing myself sing. This rule, of course, is subject to appeal if a good hatch is on three or even four hours away. Lucky for me, I live in a town that has a host of good waters and public lands less than three hours away in all directions. I like having options, though I am not crazy about the inevitable second-guessing that I am often prone to when my destination doesn't quite pan out.

Somewhere between two and two and a half hours from my garage, the mighty Big Hole is on the outer edges of my day-trip universe. I find myself pulled toward that great undammed river in the fall, when the brown trout and cottonwood trees are both colored spectacularly.

A typical Friday trip for me starts on Thursday night, when I load the car. I rig up two rods under the naked bulb that lights my garage and snake them from the trunk, through a folded-down backseat, and between the two front seats so that the tip tops rest on the dash of my Toyota. On Friday morning I wake up and go.

I stop to buy fuel (petroleum-based and caffeine-based), then point my car in more or less a straight line north toward Montana. It is September, so the mountain pass at the Montana-Idaho border is snow free and tinged with autumn. The sun got up in earnest thirty minutes ago, and now I have my sunglasses on and a Pearl Jam show rumbling through the speakers. I have found that Pearl Jam concerts are the perfect soundtrack for a drive to Montana. There are few tracks to skip, and I can sing loudly (and badly) because, well, that's rock 'n' roll, man. And PJ tends to play for a long time, so one or two shows can last the entire trip.

When I finally arrive, I immediately regret not getting out of bed an hour earlier. This is the working-class fisherman's sin: squandering the resource of time. And sleeping is squandering no matter how I painted it when I talked myself into snooze number three. Since it is a freestone stream, the great undammed Big

Hole is more susceptible to rising water temperatures than its neighbors the Madison or the Beaverhead. There is no bottom-release dam that cools the water, so the Big Hole will warm early even in September if the day is a hot one.

But its freestone nature is part of what is great about the Big Hole—no dams mean a wild river that is never penned in and tamed and rebooted through the bottom of a slab of concrete. It bends between and through high meadows and cottonwood and willow forests and cartwheels through a rock canyon. In high summer and early fall, the blue sky and cream-puff clouds look so perfect I wonder if they are staged. It is, in many ways, the exact antithesis of my small office space with fluorescent lights and a column full of wires that no one can access.

The headwaters of the Big Hole, where the river is perhaps its wildest, drop off the continental divide and run through national forest lands. Here one can drive the winding highway along the river and stop at any one of a series of pullouts, rig up a rod, and walk or scramble down to the stream. It is a public lands gem that has a passel of fish species: brookies, rainbows, even a few Arctic graylings. David Quammen wrote about the river's native grayling in his essay "Jeremy Bentham, the Pieta, and a Precious Few Grayling," a text I can't help but think of every time I fish the Big Hole. He argues that these fish expose the flaw in thinking in a strictly utilitarian manner about endangered species. If we only protect species we view as useful, Quammen proposes, we will allow the Big Hole's fluvial grayling to slip into extinction (2008). They offer no utility; even most anglers would rather catch a rainbow. And if we do let them go, Quammen notes, we will lose a specific kind of hard-won ecological variation and evolutionary adaptation, and the world will be less than what it was in ways that we can't quantify—that lack of quantification being an important part of the enterprise. The same argument can be made for our public lands, including those where the Big Hole is born, which must be viewed beyond their potential for development and monetary usefulness, beyond our ability to calculate their utility, economic or otherwise.

I haven't ventured to the upper river on this Friday. Instead I am fishing the lower river valley, which runs through another landscape emblematic of the West: irrigated hay fields and cattle range. Access to the lower river comes courtesy of Montana Game and Fish access points and the state's interminable river access law, which states that the river bed below the normal high-water mark is public land.

Even here, where the signs of humanity are piled in haystacks and bails and strung along in barbed wire, this river infuses wildness on its own terms. In the valley stretches, the riverbed is merely a guideline. In heavy water years the river makes new channels or reclaims old ones. Places where the cottonwoods and meadow grass were trying to gain a foothold are recaptured by armies of water. Snowmelt from the top of the continental divide is pulled by gravity to this place across an endless array of smooth stones under a hundred cutbanks, unearthing cottonwoods and aspens until it calms and drops and clears and I step in the shallows and feel the pulse of it adjust to my boot and flow over me, around me, against me, and with me.

I rig up and walk along the stream's edge downstream of the boat ramp where I have parked, careful to observe Montana's stream access rules. I reason that downstream is best because most of the boats should have already launched due to the heat, and I might get a lot of water to myself. In this respect I end up being right. I only see a couple of boats all day. However, the heat proves problematic, or at least that is what I tell myself as I fruitlessly cast a variety of big dries over what looks like great water for the first two hours. I have one small take, which I miss. I am sweating and a little sun-dried and wondering if I shouldn't have headed to the Madison or the Henry's Fork.

More out of desperation than anything, I switch to the nymph rod. Fly fishing has a long history of pitting dry-fly anglers against those who fish with nymphs. The sport's literature has often depicted the dry fly as a kind purity test for what it means to be a fly fisherman. Nymph anglers respond to this charge by pointing out that they often catch more fish than anyone else on the river. I don't have the same philosophical differences with nymphing that some do; I just want to catch fish on dries this day, preferably big dries like hoppers and Chernobyl ants. There were tricos flying when I started, but the fish never got on them, and my attempt to pound them up with the big stuff failed. So, nymphs. And right away the indicator jerks under, and I set the hook. There is a nice weight here and a lot of head shaking, then a disappointing lack of fire as I drag in a whitefish. Of course, this is the first fish of the day, so I can't complain too much. Whitefish are native and more at home here than we give them credit for anyway. More casting and bobbing leads to another whitey, and I move farther downstream in search of trout.

I find a stretch where the river splits and channels. One of the channels has the right depth but looks a little faster than I would like. The downstream water looks no more promising, so I decide to cast here and work my way up, mostly because I don't know what else to do. To my surprise the fast water seems to be the preferred trout hangout, and I begin catching brown trout. Most are small, but a couple run out to sixteen inches, and I find myself breathing and relaxing, focusing on the moment.

On a trip like this it's important to remember that my angling tomorrow is something of an unknown. Even though my routine says I get every other Friday, life—that wildest of creatures—might decide differently. Tomorrow may be two Fridays away or the next weekend or a month or a winter away. So each today seems more important, and each time a fishing trip seems like it might be a washout or a failure, I tense up a little and enjoy fishing less than I should. I know it's ridiculous, and I know that any day on the river is an important reconnection with moving water. I know that I should settle in and enjoy the scenery, the feel of the line shooting through the guides, the satisfaction of a good cast, the chance to live and fish in places as beautiful and rare as the Big Hole River. I know all this, and still it is easier to remember and appreciate these things after I have caught a few trout.

As evening begins to take the glare off the day, I catch a few more trout and a few more whitefish. I don't set any records, but I manage to catch some beautiful fish in a beautiful river. I eat granola on a shady gravel bar knowing I have gotten what I needed, but I am not done. I sit on the bank and re-rig the nymph rod with a larger spool and a sink-tip line. I tie on a gargantuan streamer with a name my mother wouldn't approve of, and I wade back out into the slick rocks. September is a bit early to be considered prime time for chasing hook-jawed brown trout with big streamer patterns, but it is still worth a shot. All day between casts I have been eyeing bits and pieces of water that might house a big brown: dark spots against cutbanks and behind boulders, behind piles of drifted wood, and below drop-offs where the water looks a bit of a mystery.

This is the Big Hole's secret, in many ways. Because it is not a tailwater, its fish vary more in size, much like many of Montana's rivers before we choked them with dams. A dam regulates flows and temperature, creates great habitat for certain insects—like midges and small mayflies—but lessens the variety of food available to trout and makes the river less varied in the process. The Big Hole trout have fewer midges to eat, so the fish grow more slowly than in a river like the Beaverhead. But a freestone river creates new opportunities. More small fish means more food for the truly large fish, and the Big Hole has its share of big fish. Angry brown trout that are measured in pounds don't waste their time eating insects. They spend their days holed up in the shade of cutbanks and the root balls of felled cottonwoods, waiting for this last hour of light. They spend the graveyard shift hunting, ranging up and down the river attacking trout and sculpins and whitefish. I hope to fool one before I drive home in the dark.

It takes a minute to get used to the new timing of changed line and the giant feathered hairball at the end of it. I tell myself to wait an extra beat and feel the pull that means the line has loaded on the back cast. I work on my hauls (mostly single, with some failed double attempts mixed in) and I settle into a rhythm of firing that missile of a fly at the far bank, under some brush if I can, and jerk-stripping it back to me. The light fades and all the water transforms in the flat twilight. The surface is an opaque checkerboard of dark blue and dusk white. I try to recognize those fishy spots I catalogued during the day, but the darkening land is less accessible to the eye. Shadows lengthen and details blur as night edges in.

I whip the fly against a cutbank and jerk it back out a few inches. Then, as the current picks it up, I strip again, only to feel the signature yank of a fish. It's only a grab, the hook fails to set, I see the swirl of a lost trout. It may have been a large brown, I don't know. I fish the rest of the run and get nothing. I reel up and walk back to the car, lost to that moment when I pulled the line and the line pulled back.

I spend the next two hours barely hearing Pearl Jam rumble through their set. The next Monday I wake and drive to work, park my car, and walk across the gray lot as dawn lights up the sky and renders those sulfur street lamps unnecessary. All day I think of that swirl off the bank in the dying light and calculate the hours until my next Friday.

WANDERING

Maybe he was right, the hope of roads goes on
and on.

RICHARD HUGO, "Reconsidering the Madman"

I remember the stinging cold of that first morning. Fog and
steam ghosted off the mirrored surface of a farm reservoir
that was rumored to hold large rainbow trout. Every so often
a black trout's back broke the glass surface and rolled over in
one smooth motion, adding substance to the myth. The sight
of such a fish would spread a mass of warm adrenaline through
my cold-stung appendages, and I would cast a fly in the fish's
general direction, let the fly sink, begin to strip, and hope the
line went tight. It wouldn't go tight; the cold would settle back
into my toes.

It was a lifeless, sunny cold. The sky was terribly bright—a
harsh, pale, cloudless blue so bright it seemed to be blunting
the earth. The mammoth sun didn't seem to be working at all.
It provided no warmth, just blinding brightness, hovering low
over the brown foothill horizon.

Packer and I were seventeen and loose on spring break. Perhaps some of our friends had traveled to exotic locales. Certainly
most of them were warmer than we were that morning. We
left school behind for a week in search of new knowledge. Our
research topic was roads—the sheer length of them, the unique
nature of each one, the way that some took you to places no
different than the places you wanted to get away from, and

the way others took you deep into the woods and then had the good sense to just end. We were learning that those roads—the ones that started among a crisscross of other roads bordered by cookie-cutter houses and strip malls but sped away from the gray cities and climbed switchbacks and hugged ridges and ended way off by themselves in a grove of trees where a grassless patch of earth served as a parking space—those were our favorite roads.

Packer drove a white 1986 Toyota Celica. It had two doors and a stereo that didn't work. The faded blue fake leather upholstery cracked and peeled, freeing the yellow padding through rips and holes. We stuck a boom box in the back seat, bought a twelve-pack of D batteries, and drove south from Salt Lake City in search of perfect roads that led to trout.

We knew nothing about fishing in southern Utah. If the internet was happening then, we didn't know it. We planned our itinerary using a worn copy of the Utah 1992 Fishing Regulations. We picked our waters based on one criterion: Could we fish for trout? The regulations book wasn't always clear on that question, so in some cases we guessed. Our gear splayed beneath the hatchback sun, Packer gunned the Celica south on I-15 with a dog-eared map folded rectangular between the front seats. The boom box in the backseat alternated a paradox of Run DMC and Paul Simon until we had pulled into the campground of this farm lake in the middle of the night and erected a tent by headlight.

We fished all morning, caught nothing, and eventually warmed up. Undeterred, we broke camp, climbed back in Packer's Celica, and headed farther south.

Somewhere near Cedar City we began to climb out of the rocky desert into mountain country. Trusting the map, we exited the highway and began a circuitous path through farm hills and the occasional stand of trees. We turned right, then left. The road climbed, and patches of snow and muddy puddles began to show on the sides of the road. Man-made structures mostly disappeared, except gray wooden fence posts tied together with barbed wire. We took another left onto a dirt road, figuring we were probably lost. It was there we encountered the bull.

He was large and black and snorting, drinking from a puddle of muddy snowmelt pooled in a low spot in the road. Off to the right, a cedar tree shadowed the puddle and the beast. The bull's head broke into the sunlight as he looked up from his refreshment, clearly annoyed.

He looked at us through the windshield—his eyelids half closed—then lowered his head and drank.

Packer honked the horn. The bull was unmoved.

Packer had rigged a speaker under the hood of his car and connected it to a CB radio. The speaker and CB existed so that we could easily shout at people as we drove by, something that seemed important to our seventeen-year-old sensibilities. So I pulled the Talk trigger on the CB and politely asked the bull to step aside. The bull was still unmoved.

I shouted into the handset: "C'mon, Bull, we're going fishing and you're blocking the road!"

It wasn't a particularly compelling argument.

The animal looked up again and we saw something new in his eyes, something unsettling and unmistakably dangerous. Packer reminded me casually that buffalo attacks are not particularly uncommon in Yellowstone, and although this was technically a domesticated animal, somewhere deep inside lay the genetics of a grassland-roaming beast that symbolized the beauty and the peril of wildness itself. To put it another way, this bull might put his head through the windshield. The animal eyeballed us for another moment, then went casually back to the water.

"I think I can get around him." Packer offered us a lifeline.

We edged out around the animal, the passenger tire embarking onto a patch of muddy grass. As we pulled even, the bull looked up and leaned back a little, his nose flaring in surprise.

We passed on the right, so Packer was eye to eye with the beast. Looking across him I saw a mix of fear and that same unsettling danger in the animal's eyes. I realized I wasn't terribly disappointed that Packer had unwittingly put himself between me and that bull.

The animal groaned angrily at us and feinted a half-hearted charge as Packer hit the gas and we sped off, the tires spitting grass and mud behind us, the bull shrinking defiantly in the rearview mirror.

We stayed silent for a few moments. The knowledge seeped in (perhaps for the first time) that we were uniquely vulnerable. Having traveled to this place hours from our homes and the parents who had protected us our entire lives, we could have been ended by an angry bull on a dirt road west of Cedar City. I felt weak for a moment and unsure of my place in the world. Three minutes earlier I was sure I would live forever. Now I was not.

This was a new lesson about roads: they take you places where anything can happen. Before our meeting with the bull, whenever I heard the phrase "anything can happen," my mind began cataloging lists of all the good anythings that might happen. I began to imagine ways to realize long-held dreams. But now "anything" also meant a pissed-off bull might charge your best friend's Toyota. And I knew that "anything" could also mean a lot of terrible things. It could mean drowning in a trout river or freezing to death in your sleep. I started to look at the patches of snow along the road a bit differently. My mind began to catalog all the ways the land out here might kill me.

Then Packer reached into the back and turned up the knob on the boom box. Public Enemy shouted through the speakers, and I soon felt invincibly young again.

A year later I had a similar revelation, another lesson taught by a road not far from where we had encountered the bull. This was the next spring break. Traveling north after fishing the Colorado

River near Lees Ferry in Arizona, Packer, my brother Justin, and I began the drive up a canyon toward Cedar City and ran broadside into a heavy spring snowstorm. We still had Packer's Celica, and the headlights shone right into the sideways snow, lighting up the precipitation more than the road. It got bad enough that Packer turned off the headlights and left on only the parking lights. I stuck my head intermittently out the passenger window to verify that we were still on the roadway by identifying the white line, and Justin did the same on the driver's side from the backseat. Somehow we arrived in Cedar City and found a place to buy a burger.

But in the midst of it—with those streaks of white bearing into us, plastering the windshield, the roadway filling with wet snow—I realized that we were driving blind. It was entirely possible we would veer into the canyon wall on one side or into and over the guardrail on the other. The painted center and side lines—the breadcrumbs of the highway system—were generally lost to us. We strained our eyes for the reflectors on the roadsides and managed to spot just enough to keep us centered. Even though we eventually arrived in the small college town, our teenage invincibility was no longer something we could believe in. Our safe arrival was due either to luck or divine guidance. Either way, during those thirty minutes we fought the storm up that winding canyon, we were not really in control; control had been wrested from us. Or—more accurately—the illusion of our control had been exposed. This was a sobering realization. The only difference between staying on the road and tipping over the rail and barreling to the bottom of that ravine was something outside of ourselves, something we could do nothing about. Something as ephemeral as fate or randomness, statistical noise or God's will. Something we couldn't see or touch. Something we weren't even sure existed.

This was the point in my life when I began to think about the fact that the combined forces of weather and wild country are no respecter of people. They don't care if we live or die. I always knew this logically, but now I was beginning to understand it emotionally. And that was a feeling I was not altogether prepared for.

After Packer and I left the bull to finish his afternoon cocktail, we drove that dirt road until it ended. The route took us through more ranch country and over foothills until we climbed a couple of switchback turns, entered public land, and parked on the shore of a small lake whose name I have long forgotten. Nestled in among brown rocky hills and mostly leafless aspen trees, the lake was free from wind and people. We set up camp with one eye on the glassy water looking for rising trout. We saw none.

We fished for an hour and caught nothing, saw no trout surface. We hiked the rock-strewn bank circling the lake, fished more, caught nothing, wondered about where we were, and laughed a lot. Evening dulled the light and we decided this was a pretty good place, even if the lake was barren. As we were readying ourselves for a marathon campfire, we spotted the signature rings of a rising fish, pulsing like a beacon. We scrambled along the shore rocks into range and cast toward the riser, though now the rings were gone and we couldn't be sure if this was the spot, couldn't be sure if we had seen a fish at all there in the hazy last breaths of dusk. Still we fished on with renewed vigor, this little lake offering us something we might have lost in the standoff with the bull. We fished into the darkness. Stars lit up the blackness in a trillion unique patterns. We caught nothing. We didn't care.

We had found the opposite of that fear we saw flaming in the bull's eye; we had found the hope of roads. We knew then and have never forgotten that those two ideas—hope and fear—are inexorably linked. Those places that can kill us can also show us things we cannot find elsewhere—things that will lift us and hold us in the mystery of a moment, awe us through the sheer size of a bottomless geography. We sat talking beneath that trillion-star sky and watched the flame of our campfire flicker unnamed shapes into the darkness.

The next afternoon found us at a lake near St. George, Utah. Our fishing regulations implied there were plenty of trout here, the slot limit hinting that a few big fish might exist. We had just started fishing, working our way out onto a peninsula of red rock gravel and boulders. The water was shallow and clear, the sun generating heat in a way it had failed to that first morning. It felt to us very much like the birth of a new season. We had a long drive home still to make. We felt older, more experienced, but also more aware of all the things we couldn't comprehend, hadn't identified in our limited suburban knowledge. We were becoming slightly aware of the eternity of things we didn't know, the first of which was that such things existed at all. We wondered what else was out there to surprise us.

This was a desert reservoir. A bowl of rocks in an arid country that was filled with water only because the U.S. government (with some help from the locals) had decided to build a concrete dam at one end of it. The most common foliage was sagebrush, and the rocks were dusty red and plentiful. Occasional trees dotted the shoreline. In all reality, this was a water skier's place, though we didn't see any skiers that March day.

Instead we saw a trout.

It was a single fish, cruising a few feet off the bank, swimming in some strange and beautiful pattern that took it farther along the shore on a road that only a trout or two fresh-faced teenagers could understand. The pink stripe unique to rainbow trout was clear in the shallow water. I remember it being a large fish, but that might be time and memory and hope itself fooling me. We hadn't caught a fish the entire trip. The trout meandered but seemed intent on something. It seemed to have purpose but no destination. We cast to it a dozen times, following it down the shoreline and trying to get out in front of its nomadic path. But it never moved for our flies. It never wavered. It just disappeared down the shoreline, looking for a road that took it to a place worth going, eschewing straight lines. This fish was a wanderer. Not lost—looking for something, somewhere that felt right, content that the act of traveling without sure knowledge was an end in itself.

KISSING, TELLING, AND INVISIBLE TROUT

Between my finger and my thumb
The squat pen rests; snug as a gun.

SEAMUS HEANEY, "Digging"

The river began as a trickle, no larger than a foot trail that appeared off the side of the road once we topped a pass and began to descend. Each side canyon brought more water until the trickle could be honestly referred to as a creek (or a "crick," as my dad pronounces it). Eventually the creek grew to what may safely be called a stream and, finally, into a full-fledged river.

My father remarked that it "had a lot of fall in it," meaning that it was losing elevation quickly as the water raced toward the ocean. The elevation drop created buckets behind stones and white ribbons of bubbling oxygen that snaked across the river's width and contrasted the browns and reds of the river's bed and the green stadium of pine trees lined up the inclined canyon walls. The speed of the river and the countless boulders looked to make for tricky wading. Crossing the stream would take a plan and some concentration, but it didn't seem impossible.

I was a small-time freelance writer, so small that I had another job. But small-time freelance work had led to a couple of weeks of fly fishing, under the justification of actual paying work. I thought of this as my father motored the heavy Ford van—a newer model that had none of the charm of the primer-gray van of my youth—down that dirt road in the Idaho wilderness. It was the second of two back-to-back fishing weeks. I had managed to talk the editor of a regional magazine into green-lighting two articles, and I needed photos for both. Weeks earlier I had broken the news to my wife that I would be fishing for two weeks.

"Such is the life of a working man." I spoke this sentence with a straight face. She agreed that two weeks of vacation from my actual job (meaning the job that actually pays a living wage) to chase trout and take pictures and pretend I was nineteen years old again was a good deal. Probably she just didn't want me to spend the summer brooding.

My father had found the river. He had become a reader in his old age and had stumbled on a description of the stream in a book about the Rocky Mountain backcountry written by a nineteenth-century trapper. The stream was buried deep in the wilderness of central Idaho and rumored to be full of native westslope cutthroat trout. The place was just mysterious enough to be interesting, or at least that is how I sold it to the editor of the fly-fishing magazine. He agreed to let me write a destination feature—a genre that tells you where to go and what to fish with when you get there, preferably with lots of small words and a few big photos of thick, pig-like trout that make the readers spill their lunch and drop the magazine while dialing the number of the guide shop whose advertisement smirks at them from the facing page. There would be no such pictures for this article, given that this stream had no such fish. But there would be lesser photos of lesser fish, and I needed someone to pose for the pictures, so my brother Justin and my dad offered to come. The three of us drove out of Idaho into Montana, back into Idaho again, then up a series of interconnected and vaguely signed dirt roads into the national forest for what seemed a dusty eternity until we encountered the creek—narrow as a ditch—that paralleled the road. It seemed then as if our road were the only road on the planet. This strip of national forest was bordered on both sides by wilderness areas. We were deep into some of the most remote public lands in the West.

As we motored toward a campsite, we happened on a fisher-man standing in the shallows and throwing short, tight loops behind boulders while puffing a cigar, white hair fighting out from beneath his tan fishing hat. He was the only other angler we saw that week. We slowed to chat and he took one look at me leaning out the window of my father's van and said something in a thick southern drawl that caught us all off guard.

"Did my wife send you?"

I wasn't sure how to react. Then he laughed and pointed to my ball cap, embroidered with the Georgia Tech University mascot, a yellow jacket. It turned out he was an avid supporter of the Georgia Bulldogs, and he had traveled across the country, only to find the mascot of his arch rivals bouncing down a dusty dirt road a hundred miles from the nearest town, leaning out the side window of a van.

Before we left, he took off his own hat and wiped the sweat from his shinning forehead, squinting in the afternoon sun and looking at the river. Then he said something else:

"These cutthroats, man . . ." he trailed off as he gazed at the stream. Then he looked right at us, right at me. "Don't tell any-body about this place."

I felt the sting of guilt like the barb of a fly. I was here to write about this place. I had agreed to tell everyone who wanted to listen.

I am still not sure if that was a good idea.

The first time I caught a trout that could legitimately be called a native, I was fishing a similarly wild creek at the top of a cen-tral Utah canyon. My brothers and I had fished that river in its lower stretches, but we had never continued driving up past the campgrounds where the road turned to gravel and finally ended. Here the river could be leaped across if you got a good run and a section of bank that wasn't lined by thick willows (and you were somewhere between the ages of sixteen and thirty-nine).

We had parked near a document of that river, a road sign that told the story of the Bonneville cutthroat, Utah's state fish and a species that humanity has essentially pushed to the brink of extinction. The sign mentioned that this particular stream was one of the few in the state that was home to the state's only native trout species. My brothers and I were in our twenties; we thought about this place and these fish for a few moments and said, "Hey, let's go catch one."

Looking back, our response seems counterintuitive. This species of trout is in danger of fading from existence; let's go stick a hook in one. But I would likely make the same choice today, although I would be more aware of the reasons behind my choice. Catch-and-release fishing, when practiced properly, doesn't harm many trout. Sure, a few fish die, usually when anglers leave them out of the water for extended periods so they can take photos. Most of the fish survive, though, and actually change their behavior, becoming more difficult to catch. But that is not the only reason I would make the same choice. The benefit of catching native trout—for both the trout and the angler—is that it moves the concept of a "native trout" from the realm of the abstract to the concrete.

An angler who holds a pure strain cutthroat in the very waters where its ancestors have swum and spawned and risen to caddis flies for millennia is grasping the very thing that makes these fish so important. That angler is holding a conduit to wildness. To see the way such a fish melts back into the stream—disappearing into a camouflage of river stones and sand—is to witness the products of natural selection firsthand. How many hundreds of adaptations must occur before a fish becomes invisible? Pondering such a question makes the choice of state-run fish and game agencies to plant every stream in shouting distance with non-native rainbow or brook trout seem like an entirely unnatural selection. An angler who has caught and released a pure strain cutthroat becomes an advocate for the fish and the river and the entire concept of wildness because that angler's connection with wildness is suddenly real and invaluably concrete.

My brothers and I weren't thinking of any such thing as we walked up the wet trail through the meadow grass and the willows until we found a pool of decent size. We simply wanted to catch these pure strain cutthroat because we had never caught anything like them before and because they were on a sign. And so we did. We caught several Bonneville cutthroats that seemed to appear out of nothingness as they rushed our elk hair caddis, careening over the flies in their hurried attempts to eat. Those trout were small and bright and wild, and a trophy would lie in the wet palm of one hand without danger of escape. But the size didn't matter. These fish were the heritage of our home state. They were here before we were. Before our grandparents. Before Brigham Young and the Mormon pioneers. Before Ute Indians. Suddenly, it felt important to me that they be here long after I was gone.

Back in central Idaho, on my magazine assignment, it turned out the fishing was plenty good enough to make a decent article. The fish here were bigger than their Utah cousins, but they weren't massive by any measure. They torpedoed any big bushy dry fly that slowed down long enough to be a target. And they were natives. Lewis and Clark had managed to catch westslope cutthroats while cutting a path across the Rockies and—in a move pretty indicative of the way we think about "discovery" in American history— biologists named the fish after them even though indigenous people had been catching cutthroats for thousands of years. The imperial Latin name is *Oncorhynchus clarkii lewisi*. Some *Oncorhynchus clarkii lewisi* were bright chrome with deep orange cuts beneath their jaws. Others were more green and brown or red and gold. All were perfectly beautiful and perfectly at home.

Like their native Utah cousins, they managed to disappear completely against the cobbled backdrop of the river bottom.

Never in my years of fishing have I failed to see so many fish. Those trout had spent a hundred thousand years blending into the river bottom, paying a steep, bloody price when they failed at the hands of ospreys or bears or eagles. They were a part of the river in a way I had not yet experienced. They were made of river water.

We set up in an empty campground along the road and fished lazily for a week. The weather was dry and pleasant. I took photos, fished with my dad and brother, sometimes fished alone. We drove up and down the dirt road looking for the fishiest and most photogenic stretches of water. But it didn't seem to matter; the fish came to our flies in buckets, flats, and runs—always emerging out of nothingness, always more beautiful than the fish caught just before, always slipping out of our hands back to invisibility, their existence reduced to memory and faith.

My own internal struggle that week stays with me, even though I have given up writing destination magazine articles. The practice never felt good, and I lost a good friend over the fact that I put the names of some backcountry lakes in print. As a writer new to the magazine field, destination articles were a way to break in, and I was too young to think about the implications. Most famous fly-fishing rivers need less publicity, or at least that is my current view of the topic. But I am sure the guides and outfitters who feed their families and work hard to protect the resource at the same time would disagree with me. And they might be right.

But this river wasn't a place like that. There were no guides on the river, no private property signs, and no fly shops on the banks. There were only armies of pine trees arrayed up the steep sides of the canyon and boulders of innumerable shapes and sizes funneling river water up and around in a thousand eddied currents and seams. That crystal water was as clear as summer sky and all those fish were as pristine as a distant solar system. Why would I write about a place like that? And now—having decided that destination fly-fishing journalism is a black mark on my past—why would I struggle with my choice? Why not admit that I should have capped my pen before the first word went on the page and just move on?

I suppose it's because places like that river mean so much to me now. And because I have learned that the pen is a weapon. It moves people, gets them knowing and thinking and acting. Perhaps it is an arrogant way to think of my own writing, but I find myself wondering what exactly my pen is moving them to do. Will it help or hurt? I want people to know that river exists so that they will want to protect it. That is my hope. My fear is that not enough people know about such a place, so someone somewhere with too much money and no appreciation for invisible trout will turn the whole place into a gold mine or drown it under a reservoir. But my fear is also that it will end up popular and crowded and somehow less wild; my fear is that they decide to pave the road.

Humanity has a spotty record when it comes to taking care of landscapes—not just the landscapes that we think of as wild and remote but all landscapes. We drill holes and cut down trees. We build roads that funnel water to places where it washes wildness away. We collapse mountainsides for minerals. We spill mine waste into rivers. We aren't very good at protecting things. But such negligence often happens when no one is looking, and we don't notice until it is too late. If no one writes about those wild places, how will we know to try to protect them? If we cannot see those fish, who will know they exist?

The invisibility of those trout protects them from all predators but one. Evolution cannot select such fish in the face of our distinct lack of regard for species other than ourselves. Suddenly, millions of years later, their invisibility endangers them. If we cannot see them—bright orange and chrome trout flecked with drops of sky, fish so unique and so at home as to be part of the river itself, indistinguishable from the very water that houses them—then they will remain abstract to us and easy to disregard. It is only when wildness becomes visible that we seem to appreciate it for its own sake. And yet so many wild things have spent a dozen millennia adapting in ways that make them impossible to see.

Fly anglers tend to divide fish into three categories: native, wild, and planted. Native fish have a local pedigree, a family tree that doesn't have roots in a hatchery. Wild fish are born and bred in the wild, and maybe their ancestry has called the river home for generations, but some great grandparent started the whole thing off by moving from a hatchery pen to their current location. That fish was a planter. He or she was raised in a concrete pen and air-dropped into a mountain lake or fed into a local stream via a hose and a truck.

When I consider my own personal definition for the term "wildness," this angler's distinction is useful. In his book *Horizontal Yellow*, Dan Flores writes about wanting to become native to the region he calls the near southwest. His definition of "becoming native" is to somehow attain the status of indigeneity. Such language is confusing, I think, and tends to minimize and stereotype actual indigenous cultures while raising questions about nativism and what it means to belong or not belong in a place. Instead, I think our goal should be to attain the natural awareness of wild trout. These fish behave in their environment just as most native trout do, even if their ancestors didn't. They have adapted and learned to function in the river in healthy and ecologically acceptable ways. Such wildness is something we should all aspire to.

Given these three categories—native, wild, and planter—my own personal hierarchy goes just the way you would expect—native trout are somehow more wild than wild trout, who in turn are considerably wilder than planters, who have (through no fault of their own) been raised on the piscatorial version of puppy chow in a run-down swimming pool. Putting my own arbitrary value system aside, there are relatively few hardcore chasers of native trout—anglers who want only to catch those fish that can trace their evolutionary ancestry back thousands of years to a local stream, before humanity learned fire and used it to fashion hatchery pens and fishing rods.

Sure, nearly every fly fisherman wants to catch one or two native trout so they can say they have done it, but given the choice between a bright, native twelve-inch westslope cutthroat tuned to a place over hundreds of thousands of years and a wild nineteen-inch brown trout descended from parents that rode out west on a train 150 years ago, many so-called purists—young and old—will opt for the more impressively sized offspring of immigrants. What's a hundred thousand years between friends?

I don't know why most anglers feel this way—why I sometimes feel this way—except perhaps to venture that size matters. In the end, we are all elephant hunters. Perhaps that is our own adaptation, bred into us as hunter-gatherers. Protecting native trout on the savannah of our species' youth wasn't likely to contribute to the evolutionary trump cards of impressing the ladies or help one live long enough to father more offspring, but hauling in the biggest wildebeest might do both of those things.

Still, given that our species (probably) isn't going away anytime soon, anglers might be a native trout's best hope. Native trout are a mystery in themselves. Biologists and bureaucrats have been planting fish in rivers for decades, yet they cannot replicate the native fish's connection to its home stream. Indigeneity, it turns out, cannot be engineered. In Montana, they realized that hatchery trout were so out of place in a wild river that they were damaging the wild and native fish, forcing them to change behavior in unnatural ways that no one fully understood. So they stopped planting rivers. Nature took over, fish began to adapt, and now the rivers of Montana are arguably the healthiest in the lower forty-eight. This happened in a few short years; that is all it took for trout to remember wildness. Imagine the ecological attachment between a native trout and a river that has been forged over eons. I have no way of knowing something as wild and natural as that, simply because I cannot possibly know how deeply embedded in the ecosystem that native trout is. The interconnectedness is beyond my comprehension because this is no simple machine with plug-and-play parts. And that mystery—the unending complexity of ecology, the very fact that we cannot truly know such a fish—is what makes that fish so important. And besides their value for the sheer sake of mystery, we have to acknowledge that we don't know how the loss of a native trout will harm ecological balance. We can only be sure that harm will be done. These fish are important and special—that is what makes their loss in so much of the West a tragedy.

Much of the Rocky Mountain country has lost its native trout to human mistakes. We planted rainbow trout in so many of the region's waters that the cutthroats were hybridized or competed out of existence. In other rivers, we built dams or spilled something noxious or planted a predator. The Yellowstone River, once home to the healthiest population of native cutthroats in the West, is reeling and trying to hang on to its native trout because someone with a bucket and an inflated sense of their own sporting pursuits planted lake trout in Yellowstone Lake, the body of water where many of the river's mature trout return to spawn. Lake trout are meat-eating, cutthroat-destroying killers. The National Park Service now pays commercial boats to catch and kill as many lake trout as they can, while the number of native cutthroats in the river below the lake teeters precariously toward oblivion.

As climate change strains those native trout that have survived, I feel certain that we should be asking ourselves questions that might help avoid such tragedies in the future, but I don't know the answers to many of those questions. How do we decide when wild fish should be sacrificed for natives and where—and if—hatchery fish should be planted? Can we measure native trout in time and money? Is it worth selling out to destination journalism so that a few more anglers will know these fish and perhaps fight for their survival? What if too many come to this place? What if they pave the road? These are the questions I think about and fail to answer.

Lucky for me, John Gierach provided a way to keep such questions (and a thousand others) at bay: "The solution to any problem—work, love, money, whatever—is to go fishing, and the worse the problem, the longer the trip should be" (1999, 21).

One afternoon, standing shin-deep in that central Idaho home of westslope cutthroats, Justin hooked one of the river's bigger fish— seventeen inches or so—on a streamer. I was watching from the bank as he drifted a streamer in against a log and jerk-pumped it twice. The fish came barreling out from beneath the log and attacked the fly. It was a moment of ferocity within a languid week that reinforced nature's default setting of ruthlessness. I remember thinking that I might have to learn a thing or two about streamers and what had happened just then. I also remember thinking it was the first subsurface fish I had seen all week, a fish that had let itself be seen when the reward seemed to outweigh the risk.

The last day we drove to the end of the dirt road and hiked down a well-maintained trail that led to even wilder country. The river was larger here, but the fishing was more of the same. There was a boat ramp for wilderness rafting trips, and throughout the week we had seen and heard several large rigs rattle down the dirt road with a heavy raft in tow, then rattle back up the road— louder now—with an empty trailer.

There was a guard station there, but no one was home. It was a log cabin with a corral and an outdoor faucet to fill up our water jug. It was tucked in a beautiful spot at the turn of the canyon, and I thought I could spend a summer or a year or a decade there and not feel trapped or lonesome.

Back on the river, I managed to cross and work my way upstream to a fishy-looking stretch that was a little slower and deeper than much of the water I had seen all week. Sitting on a rock I noticed stonefly casings, golden and crispy brown, sewn to the rocks, dried in the afternoon sun. The casings were almost as disguised as the trout. On first glance they seemed to be imperfections in the stone. This was a place keeping to a geologic clock. I slowed down and tied on a strike indicator (the first of the week) and a stonefly nymph. Working my way up through that run, the indicator would dart beneath the surface on each cast, and I would lift the rod tight and feel the electric current of a chunky fourteen-inch cutthroat. I fished for an hour or a week or I am still there, still casting. I fished through time and around it until I lost count of fish and hours and everything but the sound of the river and the bright side of a cutthroat thrashing in the current where a moment before and after there was nothing but the windowpane water and the rocks below, as old and haunted as the world itself.

Of that lazy week, I remember most those fish—so perfectly adapted to their life among the slick boulders. So camouflaged they may have been translucent. Fish grown symbiotic with a river, a message from the past about the ancient and powerful force of ecology, a glimpse of millennia folded over on itself, fish so elusive and fleeting they might have been ghosts, invisible except in memory and faith, but somehow concrete and pulsing alive. Perfect fish built to survive in that place for another hundred thousand years, unless we somehow manage to screw it up.

LAID OFF

We are nature, too.

Shakespeare according to JIM HARRISON

In June of 2002 I was involuntarily separated from my first job out of college. "Involuntary separation" is a human resource manager's term for being laid off. Or let go. Or canned or fired or sacked or suddenly, terrifyingly not having a job anymore. In reality, none of these words is brutal enough to describe the actual moment when one is involuntarily separated. The second you go from tethered to untethered, like a rock climber suddenly without a harness, is difficult to capture with a word suitable for either a bureaucrat or snide office banter.

I was part of the carnage of the bursting dot-com bubble of the early 2000s. My wife and I had moved to Oregon just a month or so after finishing college and less than eighteen months later I sat in my cubicle reading a terse and cryptic email from my boss asking me to attend a meeting at lunch time in a downstairs conference room that we never used.

Joe Posnanski writes that innocence "is that last moment in your life when you don't yet know that you are about to get kicked in the teeth" (2015). I suppose I walked into that meeting innocent but a bit wary. It was me and a coworker, a friend actually, though we weren't exactly hanging out on the weekends. We sat on one side of a long lacquered oak table, flanked on both sides by empty chairs. A small battalion of lawyers and managers put the table between us and then calmly relieved us of our duties and our livelihoods. They were assassins dressed as middle managers. The vice president who swung the ax said it was one of the hardest things he had ever done, but he didn't offer to switch sides of the table.

Sometimes we talk about "getting back" to nature as if nature only exists away from cities and offices, square buildings and asphalt. But in reality our civilized lives are another version of nature, a human-centric ecosystem. In this system we like to think we reward efficiency and skill, cunning and labor. I am sure that often we do reward those things. Sometimes (perhaps more often) we reward fortune and luck. It is a survival of those most fit for this gray environment, and those with money and connections are often the most fit, for better or for worse. Your average American office is a morass of survival skills and extinction; it is the Galapagos Islands with better carpet and air-conditioning and all the lizards wearing red ties or pantsuits. Humans are not separate from nature and wildness; we are another version of it.

This definition extends to our relationship with other species and the landscapes they inhabit. Human destruction of salmon and trout populations or environmental destruction of a landscape in the name of wealth accumulation isn't that much different than my experience at that oak table. My utility no longer outweighed the cost of keeping me employed. I had come to the company and rewritten most of their user documentation. They were a small company and they didn't have a lot more for me to do. I wasn't particularly useful anymore. At that point, my employment meant a lot more to me and my wife than it did to the company.

There are some who would make a similar argument about the salmon struggling up and down the Columbia and Lower Snake Rivers in effort to keep their own species from extinction or the landscapes that are protected by the fact that they belong to the public. In an age of dams and water shortages, complex shipping schedules and insecure energy, rural anxiety, and corporate farming, some might say those salmon and those landscapes should only survive if they are useful to those in power. They might say that protected landscapes need to be developed, need to turn a profit to be of any use.

Such arguments represent a cynical if perhaps occasionally necessary way to live and make choices. They resign us to the ecosystem of efficiency rather than trying to rise above it. Perhaps protecting trout and salmon is not necessarily natural in the most Darwinian sense of the word—at least in the short term. Survival of the fittest might dictate that these species have failed to adapt to the dams and competition that we, as the dominant species, have introduced. Therefore, if these fish die out, then nature has taken its course. They were not selected.

But to protect these species and landscapes, to recognize our hand in their destruction and choose not to involuntarily separate them is a profoundly human choice. It is a choice no animal bent on mere survival would make unless it was willing to admit that the consequences of losing species after species are unknowable and potentially bad for us all in a thousand possible ways, some of which have nothing whatsoever to do with utility. It is a choice of self-awareness and foresight. A choice that signals we can't possibly know the effects of our own ecological aftershocks. A choice to rise above words like "efficiency" and "adaptability" and take up a role as stewards in the hope that such a role will somehow sustain us. A choice that signals perhaps we are more than just sacks of bones and water and blood, that we, as a species, may have something bordering on an actual soul.

These ideas were not even wisps in the air during my own involuntary separation. I wore my shattered innocence on my face there in the meeting, and as I drove back to the townhouse my wife and I were renting, I probably looked as though I had just been kicked in the teeth. I completely panicked along the winding backroads through the thick forest on the south end of town. I had carved out this route to my (now former) office building to break up the monotony of my morning commute, to infuse my gray city life with more trees. Now I felt as if the thickets were closing in. I pulled over among the greenery of the Willamette Valley summer and tried not to hyperventilate.

I was a twenty-five-year-old unemployed technical writer who had just been dropkicked into a flooded job market. Two days earlier I had experienced profound joy when I learned that I was to become a father. Now I was experiencing the profound fear that I had failed my child before she was ever born. It was a quick and sheer drop from the top to the bottom—I was motion sick from the fall. How I was going to explain to my wife that I was no longer employed?

In the end my wife took it incredibly well (a few tears, but she kept her head better than I did). At some point that afternoon we decided that we should take this chance to move back to the Intermountain West. We loved Oregon, but we wanted to be closer to family. After a great adventure in the land of pine trees and perpetual rain, we saw this cruel twist of fate as a chance to go home.

My wife could see stress and thinly veiled terror printed on my features. I felt better now that we had something of a plan. But I was still scared.

"Why don't you go fishing sometime this week? Take your mind off it," she said.

So I did.

Two days later, I headed out for a coastal creek that ran through the national forest between the Willamette Valley and the Pacific Ocean. The kind of river and ecosystem I would never see in Idaho or Montana. The foliage was a thousand shades of green and the water transparent, magnifying the brown bedrock beneath. I caught some very small, very pretty native redband trout. Fish that had been around as long as the salmon and steelhead had been swimming the Columbia. Fish with a lineage older than dams and electricity, older than bureaucratic doublespeak and the divining of efficiency. Fish that had yet to be involuntary separated from their home stream tucked into a little rise of hills in western Oregon that the locals refer to as the Coastal Range.

Beyond the image of a small waterfall and some plunge pools—and brush so deep and thick that I had a hard time making my way back to the car—I don't remember many details from the trip. I remember casting up onto a thin, foamy seam that floated my orange stimulator on a curving path for just a moment, until a small trout burst from the depths and somehow hooked itself.

At some point that afternoon I remember feeling like I might just survive. I felt a little less like an endangered species.

Often I think I fish because I love the thrill of the take—the tug is the drug, as they say. Other times, I think it is the beauty of trout streams that keeps me coming back, that breathing mountain air is part of my own unique survival needs. I'd like to think I need to fish so that I can keep the rest of my life in perspective, so that the struggle of daily office life doesn't consign me to a list of those involuntarily separated from their own humanity.

But in an honest moment, I don't know why I fish.

And what's more, I know that I don't want to know. I fear that knowing why might destroy it all, make it seem pedestrian and inefficient or, worse, part of some mutation that once kept humanity at the top of the evolutionary pyramid but no longer serves any real purpose. In his book *Writing the Australian Crawl*, William Stafford warns of the dangers of overanalyzing poetry: "If you analyze it away, it's gone. It would be like boiling a watch to find out what makes it tick" (1978, 3).

I am not sure I agree with Stafford when it comes to poetry. But my gut tells me Stafford is spot-on when it comes to fly fishing. Thinking too much about why I fly fish, especially while I fly fish, is forcing knowledge in a way that cuts pleasure off at the knees. I know only that fishing provides me with something I cannot get anywhere else. And always—especially on a small brush-choked creek in western Oregon—I know that I need that thing that fishing gives me.

That knowledge is enough.

"How much faith can we put in that report? I mean, honestly, how much can we trust a fly shop report? It's their job to convince idiots like us to come and fish, buy flies, maybe hire one of their guides."

"So they obviously don't know how little money we actually have."

"Think about it objectively. They have no motivation to provide a truly accurate report. They need only provide a report that is accurate enough to keep people from refusing to go there out of disgust for their dishonesty. I mean, if they just flat-out lied about the fishing—and let's be fair, their claim that people are catching fish on size four yuk bugs seems like the kind of thing someone would make up—then perhaps people would stop going to their shop. You know, because they would be liars, and who wants to do business with liars? But beyond that, where is the motivation to give an accurate report? Their motivation is only to provide a report that makes the fishing sound better than it is at all times so more people come and spend money. They probably don't even know they are doing it, but they have to write reports that are optimistic—subconsciously optimistic at the very least, but probably totally above-board, premeditated optimism."

"Well, part of the issue is a lack of competition. I mean, where else are we going to go? There is one fly shop near the river and one back up at the lodge."

"The people behind the counter in the lodge shop don't even fly fish. One day a kid behind the counter tried to explain to me that cicadas and salmonflies could mate and produce Mormon crickets. I felt dumber having conversed with him. Like I knew less about the river coming out of that shop than I did going in."

"So who is writing the report? Some kid like that? Or the guides? It's gotta be one of the guides, right?"

"I don't know. The guides barely have time to sleep during the season, when are they going to write the fishing report?"

"So the kid or the shop owner."

"Or the owner's nephew who made the website."

"Which is why the report only gets updated once every month."

"How many Yuk Bugs did you tie?"

"A dozen. We probably need to buy more."

"We need gas."

"We're coming up on Evanston."

"Is the fireworks place open?"

"Which gas station did we stop at last time?"

"When we met the old guy who loved *Lethal Weapon* but hated Danny Glover because Danny Glover is a Democrat?"

"Yeah, where was that place?"

"The second exit, I think."

"Did they have food? I'm getting hungry."

"I don't think so. It was pretty small, but they did have a mini TV for watching *Lethal Weapon 3*."

"Joe Pesci."

"Right."

"Is he a Democrat?"

"Probably. Let's ask the old guy so he can go bananas again."

"Chris Rock isn't in that one."

"No. That might be the fourth one."

"Chris Rock is definitely a Democrat."

"I need caffeine."

"I have to take a leak."

"The thing we need to manage is our expectations. If we came into this trip with the idea that the fishing could very well be poor, but that is okay because it's still better than going to work, then any good fishing we do have feels a bit like a bonus. That is the way we used to fish, and every trip felt like a success. But now we expect too much."

"We caught too many fish."

"Yeah, and probably just one time. I mean, we had one or two good trips, then we started thinking we had the river solved. So when the river smacks us in the mouth we feel like we failed, rather than we got what we expected."

"We need to remember that we suck at this."

"Exactly."

SOLO

I hadn't really planned to fish alone that last day. It just worked out that way.

It was the third day of a four-day trip to Montana with my father and brother. We were camped on the Madison, and they had arrived four days earlier. I had only been there for the last two, having spent the first two days of the week trapped by work before I could make my way to the land of big sky and trout.

We spent those first two days as a trio fishing together. One day on the Big Hole—our first trip to that freestone river and its countless smooth dark river stones—and one day on a small wilderness lake. The fishing was inconsistent, but we were together. My father had just turned seventy, and he was making obscure comments about how he wouldn't be able to come on these trips forever—comments my brother and I didn't particularly care for. Like most sons, I think, neither of us liked considering the potential mortality of our father. My brother, for his part, was brooding at times, reflecting struggles in his life away from the river, struggles he had no interest in discussing. He was impatient and frustrated when the fishing went bad. His job had chained him to his desk for much of the past year, and he hadn't fished as much as he wanted to. I desperately wanted him to catch a big brown.

The evening after we fished the lake, we sped back across Raynolds Pass in the dying light, following a ribbon of green over the spine of the continental divide down into the rolling hills and sagebrush of the Madison River drainage. Once the cell signal was lost—ending the phone calls to our wives—we speculated on the next day's fishing. According to the anglers we had talked to that week, the fishing on the Madison was slow. Such information had led us to the Big Hole and the mountain lake. We all felt like we should fish the Madison on the last day, but my father and brother wanted to go downstream and try out some new water. I was dying to fish the wade section of the river below Quake Lake. We finally concluded that we would split up.

The next morning I rose at an hour that felt early only to find my brother gone, fishing the river near camp. While eating a stale glazed donut and taking stock of my gear, I hatched a detailed plan for the day—a plan to get far away from the ever-present Madison River crowds.

Having spent a recent week in the backcountry, I was primed to hike, and I talked my father into serving as a shuttle service. We drove in separate cars to one river access and dropped off my car. Then my dad drove me and my gear a few miles downriver to another access and let me out. The plan was to fish upstream to my car, hoping I might break away from the masses and find some unmolested water where the trout were near the banks.

It was mid-September, but the crowds were still around. Don't believe the myth that those famous Montana streams are empty after Labor Day. I think that particular legend was dreamed up by smart fly shop owners and guides hoping to keep their reservation books full for an extra month or two. Plenty of people fish the Madison (and the Big Hole and the Big Horn and the Yellowstone and most other rivers in the state) well into the fall. The only thing that really deters most fly fishermen is ice in their guides.

Well, ice and maybe a mile or two of walking. It's not really a myth that many fly fishermen in the West don't seem to want to walk. Perhaps that explains the never-ending highway migration of suvs hauling drift boats. Some people chalk it up to laziness, but I think it's something else. I think most anglers simply cannot walk past all that great water. I suppose that in order to leave good water behind, an angler must dislike fishing in a crowd enough to ignore it and put boots on the ground.

Personally, I have never felt particularly comfortable fishing too close to the car. I am always worried about a crowd of fishermen arriving in a bus or a caravan, taking all the good water for a mile in both directions. I feel better when I can get away from the parking lot. I like to range free, and on that day along the Madison, I did just that, heading up a swampy trail in the yellow-and-green meadow grass and willow trees well past the last angler I could see. My boots stamped a trail into the wet ground, and soon I was alone and suddenly felt more comfortable, more at home, less rushed. Fishing solo was something I had grown to need.

I suppose my first solo trips took place in college, in the fall of my freshman year. I didn't have a car, but I was lucky in that the river was only a fifteen-minute drive from our dorm. I would talk my roommates who did have cars into dropping me off near a campground at the bottom end of the canyon, where I would fish for hours, until someone motored in to pick me up at dark.

I would walk the river and fish the only nymphs I knew at that point in my life—hare's ears and princes. I caught few fish, and those I did fool were mostly whitefish and the occasional planter rainbow or wild brown. But the lack of fish didn't bother me too much. The green river was surrounded by a landscape of brown and gray grasses and a maze of trees. The aspen and cottonwood leaves, mostly fallen, carpeted the ground and the riverbanks. The trees walled the river off from the highway and the campground. It was quiet fishing, except for the leaves crackling beneath my felt soles and the burbling stream. I took to turning over rocks and looking for bugs. I liked the sight of a stonefly larva contorting against the air, its dark brown body blending into the wet surface of a river stone. I loved those hours alone on the river because they were the antithesis of my cramped dorm room and the bustling campus where I spent most days completely invisible to every girl in every class. At least the trout occasionally paid me attention.

As my college career evolved, so did my fishing, though it was still often a solo venture. Eventually, I got a car, and summer evenings after class found me speeding up the canyon with Bob Dylan's nasal tone humming and whining through the speakers, waders and rods stowed in the trunk. Farther up the canyon, well into the Cache National Forest, the walls receded and the canyon widened. Meadows appeared thick with willows, aspen trees, and meadow grass that turned from green to yellow by midsummer.

The river here was all pocket water beneath a canopy of quakies—the current picking its way through and over a garden of boulders, forming a thousand small eddies and pools. The fish—cutthroats now, with the occasional brown—would come quickly to bushy dry flies, the best of which was a size twelve elk hair caddis. Dump a caddis behind a boulder or on a current seam, and you were likely to be greeted by a flash of orange from the side of a trout.

This was classic pocket-water fishing—hard wading, short drifts, and bushy flies. In midsummer I learned how to pick out slots that once looked empty to my novice eyes but actually held two or even three trout. My friend Jon was a master of such water and introduced me to that place. He moved deftly up the stream, picking up a fish behind every rock and in every current seam. A few weeks later, after watching and trying to repeat his style, I was catching fish (though never as many as Jon). I found myself learning how to see what I once had missed. Suddenly, it seemed I could look at a stretch of river and know where the strikes would come, what spots were too fast or too shallow to hold fish, and what holes might bring up more than one fish. I began tying caddis flies between classes. I was hooked on that river like a trout hooked on eating grasshoppers. I found it exhilarating to know that so much of the fishing relied on knowing where the fish were and so little depended on fly selection. I began fishing that section three and four times a week, almost always alone, running my car ragged as I drove it up the canyon after class in the late afternoon and back down to my apartment once the last evening light succumbed to darkness.

The cutthroats seemed to have an endless number of ways to rise to a bushy dry fly. Head-to-tail rises, the head breaking the rough current with the mouth wide open, and even the occasional soft sipper would greet my fly until it was too dark to see, and I would stay casting, listening for the sound of a rise and setting the hook blindly, sometimes coming up solid, alone in the darkness except for the moon shining off the water and the slick midriver boulders.

I crisscrossed that section on more nights than I can remember, catching cutthroats and the occasional brookie behind every good rock and in every deep eddy and current seam. Alone in the canyon, I often felt like I had discovered some secret place that was hidden from the rest of the world.

But the fragile balance of solo fishing in that place, like any place, couldn't last forever. More and more cars appeared at each pullout, and the searching fishing—where a fisherman could range over long stretches looking for the best holes—often led anglers to fish too close to each other. I love that river dearly, but I rarely fish there now, unless work or life takes me nearby in the middle of the week. And even then, there are enough no-account college troutbums (like I was) that I rarely see the river like I used to: empty and open.

Still, when I think of that place, I remember the nights alone and the silhouetted image of a trout rising in a slick formed by a large round boulder. The light made soft by evening, and no one around for miles. That was my home water for a half dozen years. I think home water must be fished alone, at least part of the time. There was a time that I felt like I belonged on that river, like I had made a place there with three and a half dozen solo trips each summer, and many more each fall and spring. Just the river's rush and the fish.

Eventually I came to think of the Henry's Fork as home water. And to do so, I fished solo there as well.

Except for the many books on the subject, I learned the river—especially the lower river, which I can fish in the evenings after work—through time on the water alone. The Henry's Fork is a carpet of water. One look at the surface reveals very little. After a few trips I began to feel that all that pocket-water experience from college was relatively useless on a flat-water valley river like the sections of the Henry's Fork I haunted in the evenings.

I learned quickly that the easiest way to find fish was to see them rise. So I began to focus on the hatches and search for the sections of river that would light up with noses when the caddis came off, and I learned to ignore the sections that would stay silent even in a thick hatch. Fishing alone, undistracted and wading knee-deep in a river two or three times the size of the one I left back in college, I learned that much of the river was shallow and some stretches were actually too shallow and too swift to hold many fish. Still, as much as I learned—each night fishing again until after dark—the river would surprise me. At the tail end of a caddis hatch, when it was too dark to see fish rising from the road, I would stumble upon some unsuspecting piece of water that held a half a dozen rising trout, like a secret revelation. And sometimes, when it was even darker, I would find big fish rising all alone a foot off the bank in shallow water, the sound of each rise like a snare drum in the darkness.

When fishing solo with no one to ask for advice, the primary way to learn was trial and error. So each new experiment was tied to some experience of the past. In this way, I learned that the sections that held rising fish during a hatch would often surrender trout to a nymph in the hours before the hatch. And I began to discover subtle drop-offs and seams not unlike those found in pocket water, just more understated and well hidden, places that required more effort and focus—two things easy to give when fishing alone. The river taught me harshly the realities of fighting heavy rainbow trout in fast water, and even now I think back on too many fish that I never saw, that ran downstream and spit the hook, or just pulled free in the current. Like any fisherman who loses a fish, I can't help but wonder how they may have looked in the net.

All these lessons felt like my own secret fly-fishing education, though the Henry's Fork is often still a mystery to me. Many, many anglers know the river better than I do. But discovering all those things for myself, alone on the river from late afternoon until dark, made them more genuine, more personal. Fishing solo, my only companions were the river and the trout, maybe a flock of darting birds during a hatch, skipping off the water with mayflies in their beaks. I have grown to love the moodiness of the river, the way the flat water hides the secrets beneath, the current seams that are invisible until a fly rides them, slows down and swirls a bit, floating at just the right speed for a trout. I love the bright surface water of dusk, opaque from reflecting the evening sky and the silhouette of good trout in the midst of it, black on white. I strip line off the reel and cast.

That day I fished alone on the Madison, the trout came to small nymphs mostly, and I lost more fish than I landed. Still, I could pick out a nice run and count on the indicator darting under and the electric tug of a good trout when I struck. It wasn't dry flies on the Henry's Fork, but it was pleasant fishing and better than I deserved, probably. Most importantly, the fishing that day was mine. It wasn't governed by the demands of an office building full of ringing telephones and email inboxes. It was river, trout, and sky. And I drank it up.

I carried two rods—the second was rigged with a hopper and a beetle. Late in the day, after several hours of only catching fish in the deep water off shore, I spooked a couple of fish from the bank. These were big trout—at least to me they seemed large, but the trout I spook seem to grow in size as they move away from me, impossible to catch. They held in shallow water inches off the bank grass, a foot or two from the well-worn fishermen's trail. Those fish were holding there because no one had come that far upriver (or down) yet. No fisherman or pair of anglers had stomped by—talking with a fellow angler about life on or off the river—and pushed the trout out into the current. A guide on the river once told me that trout take up those bank positions in the morning and will often hold there as long as they can, until the danger is too great. Usually at the first sign of a fisherman. I had stumbled upon a chance to catch these elusive fish on dry flies.

So I walked a bit softer and slower until I spied a small pool created by some large boulders where the current evened out and quieted for a stretch of river the size of a parking space. The water near the bank was slow, almost without current, but it was deep enough to hold a good fish if one had moved in to feast on grasshoppers, ants, beetles, and whatever else happened to fall in.

My first cast was empty. On the second drift, my eyes wandered to the main current, and I thought for just a moment about whether I might take a fish on a nymph there. When I looked back to my fly, I saw the slightly hooked jaws of a brown trout protruding from the water and closing slowly on the beetle—the fly disappeared like a drowned stone.

I struck. The trout, suddenly exposed in the shallow bank water, thrashed wildly, and I was able to see the yellow belly and side. Then the fish ran for the current and the safety of the deep. A month seemed to pass while I applied steady but what I hoped was patient pressure. Eventually I urged the fish into the slow water behind me and I scooped it up in the net before it could slide downstream over a nest of submerged boulders.

The trout went eighteen inches. Not the largest fish in the river but plenty big enough for me. The rest of the day—everything before and after that fish—was like a bonus. I would have done all the walking and hiking, the early morning, just to catch that one trout.

As I moved farther upstream, I kept the same pattern—working each good hole with dries first, then nymphs. I hooked a few more thick rainbows and browns and mostly losing them in the heavy current of that famous river. I hadn't seen another fisherman in a couple of hours when I finally got close enough to the upper access (and my car) to run into a bearded fellow with hip boots and a spinning rod wristing a Rapala into a deep rapid.

I watched him for a moment and then I clipped off my flies and reeled up. I was content with a good day of fishing alone. I wanted to see my father and brother before they left the next day. So I hiked out, passing more and more fishermen as I got closer to my car. The last good hole—from which I could see my own car and a half dozen others—held three anglers in the heart of it while a couple worked the tailout.

Most of the day trips that weave together a season are solo trips for me. Most of my good friends and fishing partners live hours away or don't share my schedule. It is just me and the river, often the public landscape through which a river meanders. Sparrows. Muskrats. Osprey. I am okay with that. I like to think there are things a river will whisper quietly only if there is no one else around to listen.

THE CASE FOR INEFFICIENCY

In 1997 my brother Justin and I drove north from Utah into Idaho, veered northeast onto State Highway 20, and headed toward Yellowstone National Park. We spent the first night in a Forest Service campground in Island Park, Idaho, about twenty miles from the park's west entrance. As we set up camp for the night, I realized I had forgotten to pack a sleeping bag.

We had fished the Henry's Fork that evening—the first time I had cast a line into that famous river—and it was past dark by the time we hit the campground. I had little choice but to roll up in a blue polyethylene tarp and try to sleep. It was miserable. I suppose it would have been worse except that I was twenty-one years old and sleeping on the ground rolled up in a tarp didn't *seem* as bad to me then as it does now. The next morning, we backtracked forty miles down Highway 20 to Rexburg, Idaho, and I purchased a cheap Coleman sleeping bag at Wal-Mart. I still have that bag. One of my daughters sleeps in it when we visit my parents.

Once we got back on the highway and pointed toward Yellowstone again, we blew a tire. The spare was mounted to the bottom of the Nissan pickup's frame and we crawled underneath to find the nut holding the spare had rusted and would not budge easily. We employed various tools and cursing there on the side of Highway 20, just minutes from the world-famous Henry's Fork of the Snake River. It was midafternoon by the time we got the spare on the truck on the second day of a week-long fishing trip. We had fished for about two hours total.

Efficiency can seem like its own reward, and sometimes I think it is. There is something satisfying about removing wasted effort, wasted time, or wasted money by building a better mousetrap, by figuring out a way that is faster or cleaner. Having reduced waste and increased throughput, we are tempted to sit back and admire our work. In such cases, efficiency seems to deserve admiration, even if that admiration itself might be viewed as a kind of waste by the most efficient among us. For some, especially in America, efficiency is a kind of beauty or a form of art that should be studied and replicated—as quickly as possible, of course, so as not to waste more time being inefficient. When something works efficiently we use the language of art critics, describing it as "elegant" or even "beautiful."

At its core, efficiency removes waste. A smooth flow of traffic saves wasted time. A car that drives you places you might have walked to saves both wasted time and wasted energy. A machine that can do a human's job for half the cost saves wasted money. Right? The problem, as I see it, is that someone has to define "waste." Is the physical exertion required to walk really wasted energy? What are you using that extra time for?

When people talk about efficiency, they generally talk about saving time and money, which are theoretical goods but not always practical goods, at least not for everyone. So I—like others—have become skeptical about efficiency, or at least about the ideas that the quest for efficiency can be completed without some unintended consequences or that efficiency is an questioned good. I am not convinced we can accurately define waste, at least not in all contexts. Mostly, I am open to the idea that inefficiency has its place. If all that wasted time teaches me patience, did I waste it? If it takes me six years to get my college degree—because I "wasted" so much time fly fishing—was that really an inefficient use of my time?

These were questions I began pondering after we came home from Yellowstone, but on that second day, while we labored to remove the spare tire from the bottom of Justin's Nissan, I thought mostly about how this was time wasted, about how inefficient our trip had been so far. A forty-mile backtrack because of a forgotten sleeping bag and two hours changing a flat seemed like we were squandering our first trip to Yellowstone. It made me a bit antsy to see that precious time slipping away.

Justin and I began really fishing as a duo in college. He arrived a year ahead of me and learned to fish the local river, just fifteen or twenty minutes up the canyon from the dorm where he lived. When I arrived he knew enough about the river to reduce my learning curve. I remember one late fall day my first year when we fished near a local campground and Justin coached me through nymphing a nice run that gave up the biggest whitefish I had ever caught in my life, which wasn't saying much, but it has stuck with me. A couple of years later, after Justin switched schools and I learned the upper river, he came back for a weekend and I got to play the guide, watching him pluck cutthroats from behind boulders on a hot afternoon that slowly dissolved into a perfect evening.

But this trip to Yellowstone stands out because it was one of the first real road trips with just the two of us. I suppose that suggests that we should have expected a few hiccups because we were still learning, but we were in our early twenties; we both expected perfection. Efficient perfection.

The fishing, like those first two days, was inefficient. We were fishing new rivers, new to us anyway. And we were not catching many fish. In the years since, I have come to appreciate the process of learning a new river. It is slow and nonlinear, filled with periods in which no discernable progress is made, punctuated by epiphanies and confusion. Minutes, hours, days, whole trips can go by when a river remains mysterious and opaque. Then, a single variable might change—maybe I switch the type of water I am fishing, the weather is slightly different, or I notice aquatic insects I had missed previously—and my knowledge of the river seems to lurch forward. Sure, it stops again waiting for the next breakthrough, but it is those moments of stagnation that make the lurches so surprising and wondrous. An efficient learning model would have me getting better at a set pace, no time wasted waiting for the next leap forward. I don't think learning ever works that way. Failure is required, and sometimes that failure can be long-standing and frustrating. But I believe the learning process is a series of jerks and stops, moments of confusion that might last an interminable period before giving way to moments of clarity.

Can those moments of confusion really be considered waste? Such a definition requires some way to quantify value, some way to measure what is useful and what is wasteful. But the complexity of life suggests that any such measurement is a risk. To reduce the process of learning or the time one spends on a river to a series of components that can be judged on their own merit risks severing them from context that is indispens-able and often invisible. The complexity of an ecosystem is millions of years in the making. Human behavior is equally complex because it is saddled in all those years of evolutionary conditioning, which has resulted in the soupy, muddy mix we call culture. Can we really be sure we understand it in a way that allows us to cut and winnow using so heartless a measure as efficiency?

For an angler, efficiency can seem easy to measure using raw numbers. How many? How big? How long did it take? I used to keep a spreadsheet—perhaps the ultimate weapon in the quest for efficiency—that tracked each fish I caught and each hour I fished. The sheet performed simple division to provide me with a measure for just how often I was catching fish, a number I totaled out at the end of each year and compared with past years. I could isolate trips to specific rivers and see how much more efficient I had become at catching trout with a fly.

At some point I abandoned this practice. It seemed to me that the act of tracking such a thing said more about my identity as an angler than any numbers I came up with.

Based on popular conceptions of the word, those Yellowstone rivers were all inefficiency for Justin and I during the first few days of our trip. We drove up and fished the Gallatin River in the park and caught nothing. Justin went so far as to suggest that this river—one of the most well-known in Montana, flowing through the fly-fishing paradise known as Yellowstone National Park—probably didn't have fish in it. The next day we hiked a small stream and did only marginally better in terms of numbers, but we caught some beautiful cutthroat trout on hopper patterns in a river that was as wide as kitchen table surrounded by towering peaks and flanked by rolling parklands and brush that seemed good cover for a bear. It was a lot of walking for only a few fish, but we were settling into inefficiency now, almost expecting it, and learning to appreciate it.

Even the walking seemed to be valuable in a way that is impossible to quantify. We traded jokes, admired the world we found ourselves in, relived fish from years earlier, and laughed about the eccentricities of our parents. We came back to the car that afternoon relaxed and happy, as if the only wasted effort of the past few days had been the counting itself.

A national park like Yellowstone can feel like an exercise in inefficiency. Traffic is slow and never-ending. Hordes of cars have pulled over to photograph a single buffalo, a sight that becomes commonplace after just a few days—sometimes a few hours—in the park. The roads don't seem to take straight lines from one place to the next. Crowds show up when you least expect them, often in the form of a dozen rvs that have chosen to park on a road shoulder the width of motorcycle.

Still, you can walk a mile into the backcountry down a decent trail and leave all that behind. To do so requires you to value walking (and solitude) in a way that makes such a transaction worth the effort. Such calculations are the meat and potatoes of a course in efficiency. And that is the problem, I suppose, at least for me. I don't want to see my experience in national parks or on public lands or in waters that contain anything as beautiful and mysterious as a trout in terms of a business transaction. I don't want to measure efficiency in such places because I mistrust any attempt to calculate the value of a place as wild and complex as Yellowstone or something as unexplainable as humanity's search for happiness. It seems to me that the mere attempt at quantification somehow diminishes it.

One night we camped at the junction of the Firehole and Gibbon Rivers. This junction is the veritable birthplace of the Madison River. Near dusk we hiked up to the junction pool and fished, catching nothing. I remember the way that light died as the evening gave way to night. I remember the yellow meadow grass and the flat water eddying in a series of concentric circles. At the time I found myself wondering what we were doing wrong. But in the years that have followed I have spent so many days on the Madison that the river has come to mean something altogether different for me, and that junction pool—a place I haven't returned to but that is burned in my memory—has new meaning as well.

It is the place where the Madison River is born. The river reminds me of my father and my brothers. It reminds me of solo trips and hook-jawed browns, of wind-blown grasshoppers and caddis flying into my ears. It reminds me of dozens of evenings outside the park, miles downstream on the same river past dams and boat ramps, squinting into the darkness trying to see the rise of trout or the drift of a fly in a myriad of currents. The river means in new ways, ways I couldn't have guessed at while trying to calculate the efficiency of that fruitless night we spent not catching fish.

As darkness took the park that night, we wandered back to

our campsite while there was still a bit of fishing to be had. We were "wasting" those last specks of evening light. But then a herd of buffalo wandered in just as we arrived back at the truck. The animals alternated snorts of contempt with placid moments eating meadow grass. Park rangers did their best to keep anyone from getting gored, and I realized that most nights we would have stayed out later, fishing harder, faster, cleaner, smoother, and we would have missed this sight. I knew also that there were few places on earth where such a thing might happen, but this was one of them. Given that algebra, who can calculate whether we used our time efficiently that night?

The next day found us on the Firehole fishing a series of meadows. We raised a few fish on hoppers then managed to get a few more during an afternoon mayfly hatch. Sitting on a log tying on a new fly, I heard an odd sound and looked up to find a bison eyeing me suspiciously from across the river.

We fished hard all day, then ate dinner there in the meadow amid the splendor of Yellowstone and a blue sky. We talked and laughed, sharing a moment of clarity after days of confusion. Justin and I have shared plenty of both over the years, and I think I measure most of those days against that trip. Forgotten sleeping bags and rusted lug nuts, an overload of tourists, and (seemingly) absent trout all brought us closer as we encountered them together. I wouldn't trade any of it.

That night the caddis came off in waves. This was the first such hatch I had encountered, and I was stunned to silence. I didn't know a river could contain so many bugs. I didn't know the night sky could. Like an endless spray of tan and gray, caddis rose from the river and hovered, one cohort diving and laying eggs while another forced its way up through the surface membrane into the world of air. The water was littered with the struggle of life—caddis dead and dying and caddis being born—while the evening sky turned a brilliant orange.

But in a twist that still confuses me—still eludes the mathematics of my own finite, human understanding—only a few small trout rose, and those fish wouldn't touch our flies. We fished hard, trying every fly in our boxes, and caught only a fish or two. Then, in the evening's final movement, a large bull elk wandered down the ridge that we were facing, bugling his desire into the night. We stopped and watched until the cow that bull was after climbed to the ridge and joined him. Then the two of them disappeared over the hill.

This last summer we went back, Justin and I. We drove up into the northeast corner of the park and fished for a few days, throwing hoppers to native cutthroats. And again we eschewed efficiency. We spent a couple of hours driving each morning and evening because we had booked a cabin in Gardiner. Road construction and hordes of mammals—two and four legged—slowed our travel. No one forgot a sleeping bag, but we embraced the waste because we refused to label it as such. Or maybe because we refused labels altogether, as much as we could anyway.

Those long morning and evening drives were a chance to reconnect. Sure, we fish together two or three times a year. We see each other at family gatherings. We trade emails and text messages. But there is something about the cab of a truck and my brother and the miles between rivers that has come to mean something important to me, something that is tied up in that first trip to Yellowstone and codified by time itself, the time that has passed and the time yet to come. Those miles have meaning in a way I refuse to calculate and wouldn't know how to if I tried. Such miles are only wasted if one's view of goodness and value is altogether too narrow.

While such a conception might be scoffed at by the cold-blooded capitalist or the analyst who refuses to accept evidence that can't be measured on a spreadsheet, I believe that this view is one we must remember in the debates over public lands. We should be wary of the value system we use to evaluate public lands, no matter what that system is, because any such attempt to measure the ways public lands are important is likely to be incomplete. Not because the logic of numbers is inherently flawed but because it is inherently reductive. We should be wary of our own ability to assign value to nature, to places, to something so seemingly utilitarian as resources because such an assignment reduces the ineffable, the unexplainable to something less than what it is.

Human relationships with the land need to contain the humility that we might not or cannot understand the land well enough to label some portion of it as being wasted. Early twentieth-century foresters and land managers made this mistake. They assumed that trees and water were only valuable if they were being used by humans in very specific ways. Trees that burned in a fire and water that ran to the sea were considered wasted in the American West and still are thought of that way by a considerable population, even though science has shown that forest fires are imperative for healthy forests and that water running into the ocean supports an immensely complex system of life. The more we learn about the land the more we realize that our efforts to use land efficiently have a ripple of consequences that we can't predict. Such consequences are not limited to the nonhuman world. To me, a world of perfect efficiency sounds altogether inhuman and mechanical, terrifying even.

Yellowstone itself was formed over millions of years and required dozens of geological convergences to arrive at its present condition. In the face of such deep time, how are we to consider the concept of waste? Given that our culture tends to prioritize monetary value above other types of value, and that money is a relatively newborn concept in the long history of the planet, it behooves those considering how public lands are used to remember that value and waste are slippery, ever-changing concepts, subject to ideology and obfuscation. Doing no harm should be part of the equation when considering the fate of public lands, and sometimes that requires us to blaspheme the gospel of efficiency.

HOME WATERS

In the final phase of their spawning migration, Pacific salmon use chemical cues to identify their home river, but how they navigate from the open ocean to the correct coastal area has remained enigmatic.

N. F. PUTNAM ET AL., "Evidence for Geomagnetic Imprinting as a Homing Mechanism in Pacific Salmon"

My wife and I moved to western Oregon in the spring of 2001. I was twenty-five years old. Up to this point, I had known only small rivers. Growing up in Salt Lake, I fished the Provo River and sometimes the Green, which—before I met the rivers of Oregon—I thought was massive. Many of my most memorable angling experiences occurred on the high mountain lakes webbed together by glistening strands of water no wider than a coffee table. In college I fished a local "river" that could be crossed at just about any point and would be called a creek by many western fly anglers.

Even though it is the home of major rivers and millions of trout, the West is a dry region. Sure, we have glacial mountains and fields of snow that hold on until August (or longer), but when the snow turns to water, about half of it catches the Missouri and heads east while the other half must dodge canals and ditches, diversions and reservoirs, massive concrete dams, and other man-made water traps before it can ever see the Pacific Coast. From April to November we don't get much rain. The Northern Rockies are characterized by wide rivers and arid valleys. The rock-covered surface land is porous and hides massive aquifers of water that seeps into the earth via canals and riverbeds. A local drainage is named the Lost River because the water eventually wanders out into the desert and disappears. This is not an uncommon fate for a western river. Water here is scarce compared to the eastern half of the country, and it is becoming scarcer as climate change wrenches up the heat. Residents of the West—indigenous and otherwise—have been fighting over water since at least the nineteenth century, when easterners began to arrive uninvited en masse, declared there wasn't enough water to go around, and started damming up the place.

Western Oregon has no such problem. The landscape seemed to my wife and I to be about 50 percent water, and that was before we ever saw the ocean. Water was everywhere in small streams and giant rivers like the Columbia, which was wider than many of those mountain lakes I grew up fishing. The air was pregnant with water, an invisible vapor that made it difficult to stay dry or stop sweating. Mornings alternated between drizzled gray fogs, short-lived downpours, and occasional bursts of sunlight. Thirty-five days into my new job, after a solid month of rain, the sun broke loose of the clouds and the whole office stopped working and walked tentatively outside, shielding their eyes from the unfamiliar light to soak in vitamin D like bees drawn to pollen. Several colleagues stood with eyes closed and faces lifted toward the sun, sweet relief and gratitude showing in their countenances. My dry country upbringing hadn't prepared me for this.

My fishing skills weren't prepared either.

I made a trip or two to the North Fork of the Santiam River and another to the McKenzie River near Eugene. These rivers were wild and unpredictable, rising across parking-lot-sized gravel beds in a heavy rain then receding down to half the size, leaving the rocks clean and round as a floor of marbles. The rivers were close enough to the coast to occasionally fill with ocean-run salmon and steelhead alongside the resident, rarely sought-after trout. One night, on the North Fork of the Santiam, I climbed a steep riverbank and sat on a rock and watched as ten-pound salmon porpoised in the pool below, throwing sea lice into the wet air, dislodging eggs and roe and pent up sexual frustration. It was magnificent and unapproachable. How does one go about catching such fish with a four-weight rod and dry fly? I didn't know how to approach these rivers. I could barely crash through the overgrown brush to access the banks. I was used to trout being at the top of the food chain and the river being fordable most anywhere. I felt transient and alone.

But I kept trying. I went back to the McKenzie and caught a trout or two. I tried the Middle Fork of the Willamette, which was smaller but still large to my Utah eyes. I bought books and looked for references to trout. I frequented the local fly shops and asked after mountain streams where a fish might eat an Adams. I wasn't ready to adopt the waters of my new home until I could find something familiar to anchor myself to. I wanted one place here in this foreign land that felt familiar, even familial. My family and my wife's family, all of our friends, were seven hundred miles east. I was struggling to make myself relevant in a new job. Life tilted and swayed like the crest of a wave and I wanted to feel at home, if only for a cast or two.

Both the books and the shop sent me central, toward Bend and the Deschutes. Once we crowned the Cascades and dropped down we were back in a high desert, not so unlike Utah. Sagebrush peppered the landscape, and the sun beamed out of a sky of brilliant blue. Enamored with the landscape, my wife and I stopped and fished the Metolius River. The stream veered from black to brilliant blue and back again as it wound over a bed of volcanic rock through cedar pines and sage. Mayflies hatched and the occasional fish rose. This river was smaller than its Oregon cousins but fast and rocky. It felt vaguely home-like but still foreign. So we kept looking.

When we finally encountered the Deschutes, we found a big rugged river carving its way through the high desert. I liked it at once, but it was nearly three hours from my house and crawling with anglers and boats. We fished the salmonflies and did poorly (which is common for me). We vowed to come back but never did. I still felt itinerant.

One Saturday we found the North Fork of the Middle Fork of the Willamette. The name was a mouthful, but it had promise. We drove out through farm towns south of Eugene that looked a bit like the agricultural community where my wife and I had met and gone to school. The road crossed a covered bridge then climbed up into the western face of the Cascades until the river appeared in a canyon below us. There in midsummer the channel was bordered by two strips of white river stones from the spring's high water. It wasn't so wide that it couldn't be crossed in spots, and the overgrowth was not so thick as to swallow a person whole. The trout—beautiful cutthroats and rainbows—rose to dry flies happily. As I stood at the tail of a pool and watched a couple of trout rise to a hatch of caddis, I felt myself stop drifting and settle into a current seam. I wasn't home, but I felt steady, connected to my own life in a way that had been missing.

If I think hard about it, the entire idea of home waters can seem paradoxical. River water is transient, always moving. A river is the natural embodiment of change, the pencil that redraws the landscape in which it dwells. A river is a carver of canyons, a thief of stones and boulders and silt, a bringer of floods that can wipe out everything familiar. Rivers seem to be the opposite of home.

To complicate things further, I find that the wildest waters— those farthest from the road—often provide the strongest pull. But such places are the least like home for a creature of civilization, which I surely am. Wild places are inhospitable by nature. We as a species have tamed all the easiest places and paved over others that gave us a hint of trouble. Those wild places that are left are the ones that keep us away because they require so much effort to simply stay alive. The largest expanses of wildness left on the planet, those that are the most remote and free from buildings and roads and cell phone towers, are at the extremes of temperature. Arctic white or desert brown places that kill humans quick or slow depending on luck and skill. Most of us can't live out there for long and probably don't want to. The wild lands in moderate latitudes contain their own extremes of altitude or sheer rugged character; they court lightning storms each afternoon, and snow might fall any day of the year. We have penned the wildest animals in such places by inhabiting the other options, and we get angry when they don't stay there (and upset when they use us for food should we visit). How can such places feel like home?

Maybe because such places—high mountain ranges made of rock and gnarled bark—are sources of water. And perhaps our pull to water is some genetic remnant of our past. Maybe I feel at home knee-deep in trout streams because some ancient DNA marker links water to life. We need water to live and life begins in water. Maybe we feel at home in such places because it is a semblance of home, because our species has always needed water in order to dwell.

But that doesn't explain why I feel at home when I am alone in such places. What is home-like about sitting solitary on the bank of backcountry river or the shore of a mountain lake? Shouldn't home be filled with laughter and conversation? Wild places can be home because they are rife with a different intellectual exchange. The silence says something that cannot be repeated—that must be considered and puzzled over. It speaks to a part of me that isn't often spoken to in a gray city or even on a lonely stretch of freeway. The land converses in the feeling of wind rolling off the lake and chilling me as I sit on the shore or in the force of the current against my shins as I wade. The sound of trout rising or the way a mayfly flutters is a whisper in a library. The conversation between myself and an osprey who thinks I am catching her fish is as rich and engaging as a late-night conversation with an old friend.

Somehow these connections make me feel at home in wild places, though I know that wild places feel nothing for me. Wild places—or at least their inhabitants—care only for their survival. Fish eat insects. Birds eat fish. Foxes raid the bird's nest. Then something else, endlessly. If a brown trout grows large enough, it will eat a baby pigeon.

These places are not romantic getaways to peaceful backwaters, but at least everything in the wild is upfront about the whole affair. Maybe that is another part of it why it feels like home. Maybe I just want to be somewhere where I'm not being hustled, where the rhetoric of life is not pulling me anywhere except upstream to the next cast, the next pool, the next trout. Maybe I just want to spend time in a place where no one is trying to sell me anything. Maybe I just want to be one man in one river a hundred miles from the nearest city, trout rising in the morning light and a fly rod waving like a willow in the wind.

In some ways, home waters will always remind me of my father, who taught me to fish when I was a boy, who carried me across rivers I was too small to wade. And they remind me of my brothers—Packer included—with whom I've fished my entire life. Perhaps home waters connect me to memories of childhood by reducing my needs to those of a ten-year-old boy. There is only the daylight and some fishing to be done; the vagaries of adulthood do not exist in the bull's-eye of a trout's rise. What could feel homier than that? A return to adolescence is a journey home in some sense, and I cannot deny that the sight of expanding rings makes me feel young. Maybe this is the mystery of home waters: trout streams are a fountain of youth.

Perhaps even the cumulative memory of experience can create a place called home. If I catch enough fish from enough pools and runs, fishing with enough of my closest friends and family, then a place becomes home by default. Home is not a geographic location but a series of memories that have meaning attached to them. My memories involve rivers and trout, insects and trees.

Rivers stoke these memories of home because they are unique, yet the same, sharing traits of topography and hydrology, each one running toward the same oceans, the same salt. If I spend enough time fishing enough rivers, perhaps they all become one river, the home river.

This is the potential of public lands, which often preserve the headwaters of public waterways. Public lands make western rivers possible, and they allow western rivers to become a home for those who go looking for one. The West is known for its open spaces, and most of those spaces are defined by their aridity—the lack of water. Alternately, the *places* of the West—those geographies we imbue with memory—are often defined by water. Water congregates people and trout and wildlife and aquatic insects. With all that dry, open space, much of life is crammed into the few wet places by necessity. The fact that some of those places are literally owned by the public means that they can serve as home waters to all of us.

In Harry Middleton's memoir of growing up in the Ozarks with his grandfather and his uncle, he describes their house as a place where they prepare for fishing trips and read good books, but it is not their home. The house is simply a residence. Their home, according to Harry's Uncle Albert, is "out the back door" (1996, 43). The old men are spiritually wedded to Starlight Creek, a home river of the first order. They name the pools after Albert's dead wives. They work in the summer heat so they can fish the evening rise. They know the trout and rocks, the way the light opaques the evening surface in July. They are connected to the river and the land it traverses in some way they cannot replicate with a house.

This is the requirement for home waters: a connection that cannot be built from wood and brick. A connection that grabs and pulls you, as a trout is hooked by a fly.

When we left Oregon, I was twenty-seven. I took a job in Idaho not too far from the confluence of great trout rivers: two forks of the Snake come together less than twenty miles from our home. The locals call the smaller fork "the North Fork," but most anglers know it as the Henry's Fork. It is wide and wild, varied and fecund, full of clear cold water that leaps from the ground and more large trout than I will ever catch.

Upon arriving in Idaho, there was no internal debate about which river would serve as my home water. I had been reading about the Henry's Fork since I was fourteen. I had pilgrimaged my way to the stream several times during college. I knew the fish were tough and unforgiving. I knew that stretches of the river were wild and untamable and that others flowed seemingly docile through a patchwork of potato fields. I wanted to know all of it, every bend and wave and boulder.

In the subsequent years, Idaho has felt more like home than the evergreen Pacific Northwest did, even though I am a transplant here just as I was in Oregon. Maybe it's the aridity of the landscape, the familiar shades of brown that paint the horizons of spring and fall. Although it was beautiful, I never got used to the perpetual greens of Oregon.

I'd like to think my link to this place starts with the river, the Henry's Fork. Some of the locals here will tell you they prefer the other fork—the South Fork. They will tell you that the Henry's Fork is a river for tourists. This makes sense if you have a drift boat and an underdeveloped imagination. From May to October, the South Fork is a drift boat transport system, a veritable shipping lane for anglers wanting to head downstream. Park on the bridge at the edge of Swan Valley and you quickly lose count of how many boats have drifted by. Some of these boats are rowed by guides and some by locals. If you are lucky (or unlucky) you might see Dick Cheney.

An angler in one of these crafts is often watching an indicator and hoping for a trout to eat a stonefly nymph (a fly sometimes referred to as a "turd"), pitching a many-legged hopper-cricket hybrid at the foam line a foot off the bank, or perhaps launching streamers and stripping for the yellow gold of a large brown trout. The river gets hatches of blue wings and pale morning duns; it hosts a big fly madness when the salmonflies hatch in early or late July (depending on the year). It is—without question—a fine river and particularly well suited to a day of floating and drinking and casting and laughing. I fish it on foot in the fall, winter, and early spring when the water is low enough to wade. I sometimes sit in extremely boring meetings and shop for used drift boats on my laptop.

But the Henry's Fork calls to me, in those same meetings, in the dead of night or the dead of winter, in the early spring when ice begins to thaw. We moved to Idaho Falls in a cold and windy November. Winter set in quickly, and I didn't really fish until the next spring. One day the wind was howling a spring chinook, and I found myself wading up the lower Henry's Fork trying to understand this river's complexion. It is alluring yet mysterious, home to many personalities. The wide, flat stretches are empty canvases that offer little clue as to where an angler might cast unless trout are rising. Even then, those fish are fixed and stubborn, sometimes rising intermittently and seemingly without purpose or pattern. The canyon stretches can be ferocious and also forgiving. Drift boats float the Box Canyon like a shorter, smaller version of the South Fork catching fish on turds and tiny nymphs. The river is varied and lively, glassy and wild, home to irish-green moss, bright trout, and more bugs than a rainforest.

The fish in the Henry's Fork seem intent on surface feeding when they can. And this as much as anything else makes it feel like home to me. When I approach a section of river that stretches out like a blue plain, I scan for risers. I can see far out into the river, and I note the splashed rises of small trout thirty yards away. At those times I feel I am back in the Uintas of my youth, standing on a lake shore in the morning light, looking for rise forms or walking up the center of my home stream in college, peeking in behind the boulders and looking for fish.

Why any single wild place might feel like home remains, for me, enigmatic. But I know that my home places are pocked with rising trout. This sight calms and excites me, settles my soul and shudders me with adrenaline. I feel young and old, safe and unsure. I feel closer to those I love, yet perfectly alone, uncluttered by the responsibilities of life and completely immersed in life's essential currents. I am home.

When late nineteenth-century America was attempting to convert the remaining American Indians to the religion of capitalism and private enterprise, it passed a law that broke communal tribal lands into smaller parcels, made each of those parcels private property, and allotted them among the members of the tribe. This law—passed in 1887 and known as the Dawes Act, though it is also commonly referred to as allotment—was an attempt to instill the idea that the individual was more important than the community. Such a concept was foreign in some indigenous cultures, many of which had valued communal health over individual interests for thousands of years.

When reading Native American literature, one often encounters a deep sense of mourning for the loss for those communal lands. That loss goes well beyond the Dawes Act and extends to the massive displacement and genocide that American Indians have experienced since the arrival of Europeans more than four hundred years ago. When I consider this history in the context of public lands in the American West, I can't help but think that the Dawes Act gets it especially backward. Instead of forcing the idea of private property on indigenous populations, we might consider how the concept of communal lands engenders the idea of home. If home is a place we share—with family, friends, and anyone else that might inhabit a place, like, say, your neighbor that has different political views than you or a native cutthroat trout or a river or a caddis fly or an otter—then the communal model is an imperative. Many American Indian cultures didn't think of themselves as owning a landscape at all. To exist within a place as part of that place rather than lording over it with the power of title seems to me the healthiest definition of home.

For America as a whole to feel at home in nature would mean that America has a communal home within nature. Such a relationship requires communal lands, a commons where any member of the community can go and feel the elemental pull of natural landscapes and waterways, places where nature has not been bent to the will of the almighty dollar but remains a homeland for our species. Dan Flores notes in *Horizontal Yellow* that cultures have often set aside arid lands as public commons (1999, 137). Perhaps, then, our public lands—which are so disproportionately located in the arid West—are right at home.

HIKING CONVERSATIONS

"Hold up, I need a break."

"Good, me too."

"When did we get old? I didn't think we were old. When did this happen?"

"I think . . . ah . . . we . . ."

" . . . "

"Packer?"

" . . . "

"Sorry, I couldn't breathe and speak at the same time."

"Ah."

"Anyway, I think we should probably try playing the occasional game of basketball. Or maybe start doing some sort of physical exercise, because this is ridiculous."

"The eighteen-year-old versions of us would be ashamed. They would be disgusted with what their futures hold. They would vow to never end up like us."

"We are like walking advertisements for the dangers of laziness."

"Yeah, we are like those cigarette commercials where the old guy talks through the hole in his throat."

"We are an embarrassment."

"I was fine for the first five minutes. Then I spent the next twenty minutes wondering why we ever decided to strap on fifty pounds of gear and go climb a mountain."

"Do you think we can still make the evening rise?"

"Let's go."

"If I'm reading the map correctly, this is the junction. I mean there's the sign. It's confusing because it does not seem like we have gone far enough, but I think this has to be the junction."

"So we have gone how far?"

"Five miles."

"Wow, that wasn't so bad."

"Yeah, the first lake should be like a half mile up the trail."

"We are not as old as we thought."

"I still feel like I might puke."

"So what I do is I sort of pretend I am in the Tour de France, you know, like in the Alps portion of the race. And I try to imagine we are a breakaway group and we need to keep up the pace or else the main pack of riders will catch us. Then I put my head down and I just count the steps, and the whole time I am thinking about this being a race and I need to keep going maybe a little faster because of the pack of riders behind us. I just count to four, and then I start over. I don't know why, but I start over at four. And I don't look up, because when I do look up, I want to feel like I have gone a long way, so I force myself to keep looking down. And then finally, when I look up, it seems like I have gone a long distance since the last time I looked up. I think that helps."

"So you pretend you are in the Tour de France while we're hiking?"

"Yeah. I think it helps."

"You are a moron. You know that, right?"

"Yes."

"This is the longest half mile in history."

"Why is my pack so heavy?"

"I think we might die out here."

"What is this?"

"Another sign, why is there another sign?"

"It says the same thing as the last sign."

"So *this* is the junction?"

"Um, yes. I think so."

"So what was the deal with that last sign?"

"I don't know. Apparently, that was another junction? It's not on the map. Assuming, you know, that this is the junction. And that we didn't die somewhere back there on the trail and this is some weird version of the afterlife where we hike for eternity and keep encountering the same lousy sign."

"Why would someone do that? I mean, why wouldn't it be on the map? Don't they know that landmarks are like heroin for people carrying float tubes and way too much fishing gear up a mountain after an off-season of complete inactivity? I thought we were almost done, and then we just kept walking and climbing. I started to hope a bear would just come along and eat me so the hike would end."

"I think our eighteen-year-old selves may have put that sign up to torture us."

"Seriously that sign was a like an evil trick, like a con game perpetuated by the devil. I let my guard down. I got cocky thinking we were done. Then age and altitude and this heavy pack—plus all the hours I spent watching *The Simpsons* and eating nachos last winter—they all ganged up and kicked me in the throat."

"It was like a Jedi mind trick by the fishing gods. And we were the idiot Storm Troopers. I feel sort of violated and ashamed at the same time."

"I am going to find the cartographer that made this map and punch him in the face. But not right now, not for like a month or two after we get home, assuming we survive."

"There is still some light."

"A half mile more?"

"Theoretically."

"Let's go."

"If I see riseforms on the lake, it might just give me the energy to fish. If not, I will probably just lie down and expire."

PART TWO

REFLECTION

SHORT SEASONS

If I close my eyes now—some fourteen years later—I can hear the crunch of gravel beneath the tires as we pulled into the trailhead parking lot. I can see the afternoon clouds graying the sky as the Toyota sedan rolled to a stop. I can pick out the grain of the wooden bulletin board collaged with laminated instructions that reminded us to make sure our campfires were "Dead Out" and to "Be Bear Aware."

From where we stood—stretching after the long drive and subconsciously procrastinating the moment when we would shoulder our packs—six miles of backcountry separated us from a string of mountain lakes where we planned to spend the next day and a half.

It was just me and Packer and the extra weight we both carried on our midsections. We were twenty-six years old, and I was thirteen months married; Packer was approaching two years of wedded bliss. Our wives were feeding us three square, and we weren't playing nearly as much basketball as we had a year or so prior. More importantly, it had been a couple of summers since we had stuffed fifty-five pounds of fishing gear, food, and float tubes into our packs and trekked off toward some topographical blue wisp. Consequently, we had gotten soft. Soft and doughy.

So that six miles almost did us in. It was mostly uphill, and somewhere around mile five I started to wonder what had happened to my invincible youth. As we topped the final ridge to drink in that exhilarating view of the first lake—won through a long, hard climb—I found I could only enjoy it for a moment because I was pretty sure I was going to die.

I stared at the water and the rings of rising trout. I was shamefully aware that I had entered the Uinta Mountains—one of my favorite places on earth—yet I had no desire to string up my rod. I wanted only to shed my pack and sit down, to drink as much water as my belly would hold, and pass into sweet unconsciousness.

We pitched our tent and cooked dinner in the dying evening light. Then we crawled off to a black sleep.

I have known Packer since we were two years old. I don't remember how the two-year-old versions of me and Packer were introduced. He has just always been there. I don't know an existence without Packer. We were neighbors. He lived three houses down, across the gravel road that separated and connected the old brick homes between Redwood Road and Old Man Pershon's alfalfa field. We played the '86 Super Bowl out in Packer's backyard. We rode his giant dog like a horse. We raced matchbox cars down the slide of his swing set. I was there the day he tore a gash into his thigh on an exposed bolt while running up the same slide and jumping down the ladder. I remember the surprise on his face turning to pain, the blood flowering in the wound and running down his knee and calf. He didn't speak or even cry out; he just rushed inside the house and pulled the screen door closed behind him. I stood in the backyard and stared at the door, then looked up at the gray sky, then down at the grass. I inspected the slide to see if I could figure out the crime scene. Then I walked home.

In fourth grade, Packer moved from the west side of the Salt Lake Valley to the east and began attending a different school. In the weeks leading up to the move, I was inconsolable. It was one of the more traumatic moments of my childhood, which probably says a lot about the cushy life I was born into.

Packer and I stayed in touch thanks to parents who were willing to make a ridiculous number of trips across town for the sake of their kids. We played soccer on the same teams, traded Christmas presents, and stayed as close as we could living twenty-five minutes apart in the age of the bicycle rather than the age of the smartphone.

We were city friends, really—which makes the fact that we ended up connected by mountains something of a mystery. All those boyhood memories took place in a gray city. But we were both Boy Scouts, and our respective Boy Scout troops spent time in the mountains. I think we each felt a connection to the mountains relatively young. I don't think these connections were a coincidence. Packer and I were and are so alike that his having a guttural connection to wild places was not surprising. Rather, it may have only been surprising if he had *not* wanted to explore the woods, had not felt at home in high mountains, because I loved such places and he was just a different version of me, especially then. It felt perfectly natural that Packer—who besides me had only sisters—wanted to go with my dad and my brothers and me to the Uinta Mountains and cast spinning rods into the pine-gated lakes. So my dad consented to bring him along. We hopped from rock to rock along the lake shores and fired arcing casts into the deep blue reflections of the sky. Packer's lure of choice was this giant Blue Fox Spinner contraption that claimed to attract fish through subsurface sound waves. I trusted a Mepps golden blade spinner, with red spots, size zero (the smallest). The fish weren't much bigger. We used a fly and bubble when the fish were rising. We used two-pound test Stren line bought from the local hardware store.

We didn't know it then, but we were in a place so wild and free and perfect for teenage boys that we felt at ease. We had not yet learned that wildness could injure us. We had not yet learned that civilization could soften us. If I could talk to those boys on the banks of those lakes—the younger versions of me and Packer—and tell them that they would grow into men who returned together to those same lakes doing more or less the same things, those boys would nod without surprise.

"Of course, that is what happens," I think they would say. "What else is there?"

The morning after the six-mile walk that nearly killed us, I overslept and woke to find Packer kicking back to shore in a half-inflated float tube. Sometime during the last two years, his tube bladder had developed a leak, and he was just learning of it now as his float tube spit bubbles into the water at an alarming rate.

For the first time, I really took in our surroundings: a green lake circled by an audience of pines, a deep blue sky flecked by a few stray white clouds and fringed by gray, snow-spotted peaks to the west. Those six miles from the previous day were still present in my shoulders and hips, but I was ready to fish.

As Packer tried unsuccessfully to use wader repair glue to mend his tube, I managed to get my own tube blown up and a rod rigged. I bobbed out onto the lake and began catching pan-sized cutthroats relatively quickly. Only a couple of intermittent riseforms broke up the lake's morning glass, but it never took long for a small cutthroat to locate my dry fly and attack it with abandon. This is the reality for mountain trout: they must eat when they get the chance. Couple the high country's short summer with waters that have too many trout and not enough insects, and it can sometimes feel as if the fish are queued up, noses pointing skyward, eyes on the surface, waiting for a fly to land so they might race to it. The fish were easy and beautiful— like a reward for yesterday's work. After a couple of hours on the water, I let poor, tubeless Packer kick around in my tube while I made breakfast, then we headed out across the basin, climbing the meandering mountain steps up toward the higher lakes.

I was fourteen when I got serious about fly fishing, as serious as a fourteen-year-old can get anyway. My father taught me to cast in the backyard, aiming at a one-gallon bucket with a piece of yarn tied to the end of my line. By the time we learned to drive,

I had talked Packer into buying a fly rod, and he had learned to cast the thing, sort of. Packer's 1986 Toyota Celica was my first fishing car, even though it didn't belong to me. The car opened up a new world to us. We spent summer weekends in the Uintas or at Strawberry Reservoir, camping and fishing. If this was some kind of summer school, the mountain roads and trails became our hallways, the lakes and creeks our classrooms.

We were crazy for the mountains. One year we wanted to feel the mountain air so badly that we headed up the Mirror Lake Highway with another friend on Memorial Day weekend. We ran into piles of snow long before the turn off to the first lake. So we drove down and camped in the meadows of the upper Provo River. By then it was dark, and all three of us fell in the swollen river trying to determine if we might be able to fish that night. We built a huge campfire to dry off and stayed up all night. The next day I flicked ice and water at Packer's face in an attempt to keep him awake while he drove down Parley's Canyon. We made it to Strawberry Reservoir by noon.

A mountain weekend for us in those days meant a Friday evening drive to the trailhead—arriving late because Packer's girlfriend (now wife) had delayed him with her girlish wiles—then a hike that started lit by the soft light of dusk but ended in moonlight. We would hike without flashlights, letting our eyes adjust to the darkness until picking out the trail was easy. Even in the moonlight, the lakes stood out. We would hear the waves lapping up the shoreline, feel the cool air blowing off the surface, smell the water, and know we had arrived. We set up the tent using flashlights, then piled in and stayed up even later talking about fishing, sports, and girls. The next morning, we would stumble out bleary-eyed and dehydrated, looking for a wooden wilderness sign to let us know if we had managed to find the lake we were aiming for or if we had happened on some other body of water in the dark.

I can think of no time in my life when I felt more at ease than I did as a teenager in those mountains. We were ridiculously over-confident. We'd hike into remote lakes without any food, planning to eat fish we had yet to catch. Our raingear was substandard, our tents mediocre at best. We survived on a combination of good fortune, ignorance, and youth. We were painted by those days and nights in the mountains, shaped and conditioned by the peaks and the trout, the lily pads along the lake shores and the wildflowers in the meadows. Even now I turn to my memories of those days to escape people and moments that would tear me down and rebuild me into something I don't recognize, something out of place in the granite edges, the gnarled junipers, the spongy tundra of the high country. If we are a construct of our experiences, then my foundation was laid along winding trails through wildflower meadows surrounded by mountains, ten thousand feet up and a thousand miles east of the Pacific, a mirrored lake in the distance, the setting sun cradled in the saddle of two peaks.

Two things I love about the high mountain backcountry are the way the lakes are grouped like families and the way streams bind those lakes together. Those bright rivulets racing over gravel and through deadfall—often no wider than an irrigation ditch but a thousand times more wild—are the veins of the wilderness, bringing life with them. And seemingly each time such a stream runs into a low spot or drops off a ridge, it forms a high-country lake.

As creatures of the low country, we start at the bottom of such streams, so the story of water seems to happen in reverse. We trail up a creek and watch the water get smaller. We climb a ridge and break out of the trees to discover the vast mirrored expanse where a small stream has filled some ancient granite bowl. But for the creek, the journey starts up high—way above the trees among the mossy tundra grass, shale rock, and sky. Vast snow fields pinned to mountainsides trickle out threads of water that gravity weaves together. When enough threads are joined, a creek is born. When that creek rumbles into a rock bowl, it pools up into a mountain lake, brilliant mirrored blue against the dull unforgiving gray of the highland rocks and the mysterious deep greens of the trees.

After breakfast, we left our camp and followed the small inlet stream up through a wandering mile of pine trees, rocks, and deadfall until we found the second lake in the basin—the unimaginatively named Circle Lake—and more eager pan-sized cutthroats. I let Packer take the tube, and I cast along the shoreline and scouted the stream above the lake.

When he was done, I was anxious to fish the creek. There above the second lake, the water sliced its way through a meadow, and trout rose eagerly in the pools. The sky was a brilliant mix of clouds and blue. It was early August, and the mountains were at the height of their glory. A dozen shades of wildflowers—whites and purples, deep oranges and reds—accented the meadow grass. I stood back from the creek with the float tube strapped to my back and cast over a high bank into the top of a flat. The first trout came quickly in a mad rush to beat his river mates to an elk hair caddis. I lifted the thin eight-inch trout out of the water to avoid spooking the rest of the fish, but I don't think it mattered. The short season left those fish with little choice but to eat something as substantial as a big caddis.

For the next several hours, we took turns catching fish as we worked our way up through the meadow toward the third lake. I caught a fourteen-inch cutthroat where the creek exited the lake, a veritable trophy for a Uinta creek that was no wider than the cramped hallways of my newlywed apartment. It was there we got our first good view of lake number three. A few patches of pine trees stood out along the lake's shore, and a massive boulder field climbed the sky opposite us. We were at the edge of timberline here. We could see patches of snow holding onto winter as the world sloped higher. The trail rounded the lake and rose along the edge of the boulder field, climbing toward a fourth lake—which was nothing to us then but a blue spot among the brown topographical curves of our map.

The summer between high school and college, we spent two full weeks and several long weekends in the mountains. We hiked thirteen miles into a basin with a half dozen lakes and caught artic grayling on dry flies—when those fish rose to a Griffith's gnat, their dorsal fins broke the surface like a shark circling a life raft. We waited out a dozen rainstorms and slept in puddles. We felt the sick taste of lightning striking close, the clap of thunder in our back teeth.

Near the end of the summer, we drove a winding dirt road on the northeastern slope of the Uintas, looking for a remote trailhead and hoping we would have enough gas to make it back to town four days later. When we finally found the trailhead, the register told us that someone named Trey Drinkard belonged to the dusty-blue pickup parked next to Packer's Toyota. We met him a few miles up the trail. He was wearing the biggest pack I had ever seen, and he was carrying a full daypack in each hand. The upside down V of a compound bow peaked out the top of one day pack.

"Elk hunt starts next week. This week I'm just scouting," he told us.

He went on to explain that if he did kill an elk—back here in the woods, miles from his vehicle—he expected it would take six trips to get it out: four for the meat, one for the rack, and one more for all his gear.

We decided that we were not as tough as we thought and that Trey Drinkard might be the wildest creature we had ever encountered in the Uintas. We passed him and walked the twelve miles up a stone-pocked trail to a basin of blue lakes painted on green meadows at the foot of a massive gneiss peak named after someone called Gilbert. This place was part of the guts of the Uintas. That peak was part of the spinal ridge that runs along the center of the range forming a ragged line from east to west, starting in Utah and ending in Wyoming.

The Uintas are the only major Rocky Mountain range that runs east to west rather than north to south. The High Uintas Wilderness was established in 1984—when Packer and I were eight years old—under the Wilderness Act that Wallace Stegner argued for in his famous Wilderness Letter. The wilderness includes more than 450,000 acres, the highest mountains in Utah, and mile upon mile of backcountry trails. The mountain range is the birthplace of the Provo and Duchesne Rivers and major tributaries to the Green River, itself a tributary of the Colorado, one of the major arteries of the American West and one of the most contested (and dammed) rivers on the planet. More than five hundred miles of trails crisscross the Uintas. The mountains are home to more than a thousand lakes and back then—at eighteen years old and having knocked out twelve miles without really getting past third gear—we thought it wasn't out of the question that we might one day fish every single one of them, that we might hike all of those miles of trail. Those lakes and that entire spinal ridge of peaks lie inside wilderness boundaries, meaning that the only way in and out was via sweat and sore feet, but given that the land was public, they were open to anyone who could make the journey.

Some people came in on horses, and occasionally we encountered a llama group on our travels, but the more you got to know the mountains the easier it was not to see anyone at all—except the occasional Trey Drinkard. This basin was a long way from the main highway and from any town of reasonable size. Just driving to the trailhead was a commitment. I once heard of backpackers in the Wind River Range queuing up for campsites in popular areas, waiting for groups to leave so that new groups could check in and tent up, like some sort of backcountry hotel system. These meadows and lakes at the base of Gilbert Peak were not that kind of place, unless you were a moose.

A day after we met Trey Drinkard, the moose came in the evening to the meadow lake where we were camped as if someone had called a meeting. A group of five or six came down a hill of pine trees and ran Packer off a pod of rising fish. Then another group of moose came up the same trail we had hiked in on. Between the two groups there were twelve or thirteen moose, including several wide-racked bulls that waded out into the shallow lake and began calling. We retired to our campsite and watched as the males crashed horns. The moose exited as couples, male and female. The big animals didn't pay us much attention, but we were keenly aware that they could have gored us easily. Luckily, even though we were eighteen and full of vinegar, we had no interest in their women.

We built up a big fire and stayed up late, listening to moose calls and telling stories. All day we had caught fish and mostly stayed dry. For one night, we felt part of those mountains rather than just visitors. All those moose—the horns cracking like mountain thunder, the long walk of moose courtship, the rut sounds like a backward record, the sunlight fading and fish rising. The mountains were revealing something we hadn't seen before. Something only those with patience, luck, and worn hiking boots could see. Talking over the fire, eating granola and Mike and Ikes, the eighteen-year-old versions of us agreed that we were in the midst of something special. It went unsaid, but those boys were confident that trips like that would happen forever.

Back at that third lake—eight years after we met Trey Drinkard—the twenty-six-year-old versions of me and Packer unhitched the tube from my back. I strapped black fins over my boots, stepped into the tube, and waddled down to the lake's shore. As I kicked out onto the lake I cast a glance at the storm clouds coming over the peaks. The clouds grayed, and I kicked hard and trolled a woolly bugger. Halfway out a good fish struck. It was a much thicker trout than the one I had released in the creek. We needed dinner, so I smashed the trout's skull with the butt of my rod, zipped it into a pocket of the tube, and commenced fishing.

Then I heard the first crack of thunder.

Another look at the fast approaching thunderhead sent me back toward shore, kicking harder. Looking back now, I realize I was at a unique point in my life: old enough (and smart enough) to drive several hours and hike to a place full of beauty and wild trout but fraught with brutal forces that cared nothing for whether I survived, yet still young enough (and dumb enough) to have kicked out onto the lake among the gathering clouds with hardly a second thought.

When I reached shore, I kicked off the flippers, and Packer and I scurried into a stand of pine trees as rain and hail began to pelt us. Lightning followed, and we wondered if a stand of trees was the best place for cover. We decided that we weren't sitting under the tallest trees in the area (which seemed like a good thing) and that there wasn't really anywhere else to go (which made us feel a bit helpless).

I have sat through dozens of lightning storms in the backwoods, but this one stands out for the ferocity and closeness of the strikes, for the violent cracks of thunder, the smell of ozone and rain, and the freezing hail that lashed us with cold. The whole storm lasted the better part of twenty-five minutes, but it felt like a month huddled there in the brush, making nervous jokes about how our charred carcasses would be cooked just right for a bear.

We talked about what to do next, agreeing that—when it was safe to travel across open country again—we ought to make for camp and cook dinner, get ready to fish the evening, and prepare for our hike out in the morning. As with most of our conversations, the talk made its way to fishing. We talked about how we would like to fish that fourth lake up beyond the ridge. We picked out the trail and guessed at how long it would take and whether we could camp there. The Forest Service literature implied that lake was deep. We imagined a place where a few large trout might reside, swimming undisturbed except for once or twice a year when some ambitious angler made the trek up through the rocks.

Eventually, the lightning rumbled off toward the interior peaks but left the rain behind. Packer and I huddled in the trees, watching the rain and talking about fishing.

What we didn't talk about—but what I think about now as I close my eyes and see that place so clearly—is that we might never make it back. We were in our own short season. We were young men with enough strength to switchback our way into the mountains carrying heavy packs full of too much fishing gear and not enough food. We had enough free time to spend a couple of days in the woods chasing trout and not enough grown-up responsibilities to make us think we had something better to do. We had no idea that would soon end.

Less than a year later, Packer would hold a newborn daughter in his arms. He would take a job as a junior engineer for a semi-dysfunctional engineering firm that had eight employees. He would provide for that child and the children that followed by working until he owned that company.

My life was different but the same. Over the next year, I graduated college, took a job with a software company in Oregon, and lasted just long enough to build a résumé and fish a few famous rivers before the dot-com bubble left me jobless in a place that didn't quite feel like home. So my wife and I moved back to the Rockies and had kids of our own. I found one big job and three or four little ones that ate up my time like those mountain cutthroats taking caddis flies.

And although we were disgusted by the dying embers of our never-stop-hiking youth, both Packer and I continued to grow softer and doughier as we got older. Strength, time, and responsibility started working against us rather than for us. Our short season was ending.

Of course, we knew none of this as the rain turned to mist and we gathered our wet gear for the trudge back to camp. Along the trail, we encountered a wilderness ranger on a horse. He asked about the tent he had seen back at the first lake—was it ours? It was. He informed us we would have to move it two hundred feet from the trail per wilderness regulations. As he rode off, we thought about the rocky ground away from the trail and how we had looked for a tent spot there originally but couldn't find one among the boulders.

We grumbled as we trudged on, thinking about moving our camp while everything was still wet. Back at the first lake, a Boy Scout troop had set up camp close enough that we could hear their campfire talk. And over the granite peaks we could see lightning flaring up again, readying to batter the basin a second time.

We decided it was time to leave the mountains.

I walked over and donated my trout to the Scouts' dinner, and Packer began breaking camp. We gave no thought to when we might return and scramble up the gravel and shale to that fourth lake, made no plans of when we might come back to that basin at all. We just assumed we would come back, but we haven't.

Some nights I dream of the basin's artery—that small creek teeming with eager cutthroats. I can see the trail snaking its way up through the boulders as I sit in the trees. I can smell the lightning. Some days, while the thirty-eight-year-old version of me is trapped in my office at work, I pull out the dog-eared map I keep tucked in a desk drawer and gaze at the name and shape of that fourth lake. I count the topo lines and look hard into the blue. Once—while stuck in traffic on the way home from the office—I called Packer and we talked vaguely about the whole thing. We hung up no closer to that lake than before. Of course, on that gray evening thirteen years ago as we broke camp, all that was in the future.

Back then we knew only that we had had a great day. That wild trout and mountains were still within our reach. And that if we hustled, we might get out before the rain started again. We didn't think twice. We slung those packs onto our aching shoulders and hips. With thunder and darkness chasing us, we raced down the mountain back to the car and went looking for the nearest place to get a burger.

THE BANK GRASS

Justin and I were way upstream from the car—maybe a mile and a half—making sure to stay in the river. A sign on the bank told us in bold, dark letters that leaving the river here would constitute trespassing, and violators would be prosecuted.

In 1985 Montana's state legislature passed a law that made our access that day legal and dictated the language of the sign. Montana's law, which is the envy of anglers throughout the West, states that access within a river's "ordinary high water mark" is legal for "recreational use" (Montana Department of Fish, Wildlife and Parks, n.d.). Importantly, this access opens up some of the wildest, most biologically diverse places in all of Montana to anglers, kayakers, and other recreationalists.

It also serves as a reasonable example of two sides with opposing interests figuring out how to work together. While there have been legal dustups in the years since the law was put in place, and while the language on that sign seemed rather ominous to us that day, for the most part river users and landowners have learned how to coexist. Montana landowners haven't led an armed occupation of public boat ramps on the Madison to protest the law, and anglers haven't tried to forcefully acquire private land for fishing. Sure, the truce is a bit uneasy at times, but the two sides seem to manage.

About a third of the way out from the sign, there was an island that split the river into two unequal channels. The smaller channel was framed on the shoreside by a grassy undercut bank. We had kicked up some hoppers along the banks as we walked before we encountered the sign. So I was standing in the smaller channel casting mindlessly against the grass, trying to see just how close I could pitch my hopper into that black strip of water that borders a cutbank. Two inches from the grass, an inch, then into the grass itself, and back out with a slight tug. I caught one small fish at the back end of the channel, but it looked too shallow and fast when I got to the top, so I waded up past the island through the heavy current to what looked like better water.

The current slowed and deepened as I positioned myself downstream of a boulder, right along the bank, and cast into the current seam behind the boulder—one perfect drift, then a dozen. I worked the water on either side of the boulder, then the slick just above the rock—the place where fish sometimes hold, grabbing bugs just before they slide off the plate. I made cast after cast after cast. It was too hot, I figured. It was only ten in the morning and already the sun was cooking us.

I woke from my heat-induced daze to the far-off sound of my brother's voice. I looked downstream to see his rod bent. He was standing in the shallows near the island, and the fish was up against that grassy bank.

He was less than sixty yards away and yelling, but the river noise made the words sound like a distant call: "Bring the camera and the net!"

I splashed my way downstream, mindful not to get out onto the bank and run, careful not to break my ankle by sticking my foot between two of those bowling-ball-shaped Madison River rocks. I made it out to the shallow water above the island, half-ran to the dry land, and stashed my rod on the island bank as Justin walked the fish downstream.

He had risked jinxing the fish by asking for the camera, so I knew it was big. He was talking while he fought it, and I hadn't yet seen the trout.

"I caught it right at the top of the channel. Water couldn't have been more than ten inches deep. He ate the hopper. It was only an inch or two off the bank."

Ah, yes. I knew the spot. I had skipped that water. Why? Because it was too shallow to hold a nice fish. I am an idiot.

He continued: "When I hooked it, it went crazy, nearly jumped out onto the bank."

"Good thing it didn't, or else it would have been trespassing," I joked.

He finally guided the big brown into the shallows and I got a good look at it. It was beautiful. I positioned myself downstream, and the fish tried in vain to head back toward the far bank, away from us. But Justin kept working it, swimming the fish with the current back toward the island until the head was out of the water for a moment. I slid the net under the fish's ample belly and came up with a log of brown trout.

It taped at just over twenty inches long. I took photos of the fish in the water as my brother extracted the hopper from its jaw. I took more photos as he held it up for a moment, his smile as wide as that Montana sky. I took a few more photos as he slipped it back in the stream.

It was a buttery yellow split pine of a fish. Fat and colorful and spots without number. The light was late morning, and the fish was majestic, resting in the shallows, gills opening and closing like a respirator. The light sparkling off the water and the dorsal fin. The sky so blue and the bank grass so green and yellow.

Justin slowly loosened his grip, and the trout pensively finned out into the current, blending in with the boulders. It edged farther out into the current until it became just another river stone.

About the stream access law, Montana's Department of Fish, Wildlife and Parks has noted, "no amount of legislative action or rulemaking can do more to promote harmony between landowners and recreationists than the individual actions of the parties concerned. Because the success or failure of the law hinges on the behavior of the landowners and recreationists, we cannot over-emphasize the need for cooperation and mutual respect" (n.d.).

It is this mutual respect that seems most tenuous in today's political climate and serves as perhaps the lynchpin to managing public lands in the West—respect for the other side, for the landscapes themselves, for the desire of local residents to make a living, for the considerations of indigenous populations and their conceptions of the landscape as sacred, and for the intrinsic value of all of these things. For an angler, it is also respect for the brown trout that move into shallow water near a grassy bank and wait for falling grasshoppers. Respect is often evinced by civility and honesty, both of which seem to be in short supply in discussions about public lands.

But the riverbeds of Montana streams can serve as a kind of geography of hope all their own. These riverscapes represent the hope that those who disagree might struggle their way to a compromise. For all its cultural associations with rugged individualism, the American West has at times hosted agreements among diverse interests in regard to the land itself. Consider the states who managed to hammer out the Colorado River Compact, a flawed agreement perhaps but one that has more or less kept the peace in regard to the most sought-after water in the West for more than eighty years. Such compromises are essential to land use in a dry country where most citizens want to keep the public lands public. In her book *Where Land and Water Meet*, environmental historian Nancy Langston suggests that solutions to land and water issues in the American West can come through compromises, "and those compromises become possible when people are willing to shift their identities and find common ground with former enemies" (2003, 165).

THE GLIMPSE

There are only a few things I am sure about from that morning. I remember most vividly the moment when I got a look at the thing. I was shin-deep in the Henry's Fork, water reflecting the sun, my rod skyward and arching, the line pulled tight. The fish moved out of the seam and swam exposed for a millisecond. I got my glimpse.

It was only a moment, but there was one feature I could not miss. This fish was . . . big. I know that is a poor adjective. No self-respecting writer should lean on a word so plain and monosyllabic. But I find myself returning to that irreplaceable description: *big*. When I got my glimpse, the word rose in my mind and surfaced: "Oh my, that's a big fish."

I had arrived expecting pale morning duns. A few trout rose, but drag-free drifts with proven pale morning dun (PMD) patterns went untouched. So I knotted on an X-caddis, and a few small fish took the fly with splashy rises. I switched to a bead head caddis pupa and an indicator, hoping to catch something of size.

Several nice trout came to the new fly quickly. The best was a fat rainbow that raced downstream and tested my knots but eventually ended up in the net. The sun was up high, and the fish shone, the pink streak along its side rising with its gills as I gave it back to the river. Two casts later—in the same current seam—the white yarn indicator jerked to a halt and submerged. I raised the rod and set the hook on something with no give whatsoever. I had been hooking fish for thirty minutes, but I still thought I had snagged a boulder—until it began to swim.

Large fish threaten my sanity. A true trophy is rare enough that, once I realize what is happening, I immediately begin to wonder how I will screw it up. After I got the glimpse, I reeled up the slack and waited for a run. Each second of waiting brought an unsettling internal spool of fear tangled with excitement and a little dread. There were only two potential outcomes, and only one was worth considering.

It is strange really, the importance anglers place on having a truly heavy fish—be it trout or tarpon—in our hands. While small fish are counted even when they spit the hook ten yards away, we have not caught a big fish until we have touched it— felt the wet scales against our fingertips. To hook even one such fish is to know the fear of failing in sight of the finish. In some twisted, anxiety-ridden way, losing a huge fish seems worse than not hooking the fish at all.

It has been nearly five years since the moment I glimpsed that fish. In that time, I may have tricked myself. Maybe I can't trust my mind because of what happened next. Probably, my memory has grown the fish with each mental viewing. Maybe it wasn't that big. Maybe it was a whitefish. But maybe it was a trout. Maybe my mind has made that fish—and that day with the caddis and no PMDS—something it was not.

Maybe.

I knew only in that moment what I still know—that I was hooked to something big. Bigger and in some way wilder than anything I had hooked before. I was exhilarated and afraid.

The thing didn't stay put. It labored upstream like a train— slow at first but gaining momentum and speed until I was just a passenger, powerless to turn it or slow it down. Line sang off my reel like a church choir. I stood helpless, palming the reel lightly and waiting for the backing knot.

Then—without a leap or an abrupt jerk—the line went limp.

Reeling in, I found that the hook was not straight and that no knot had given way. The fly—my number fourteen bead head caddis pupa with partridge legs—had simply pulled free.

A few hours later, I stopped shaking.

GOLDEN

Perhaps the golden trout first swam into my brain during my youth—all those days among the snow-painted peaks and alpine lakes in the High Uintas Wilderness. I have read that the Uintas are home to a few goldens, deep in the roadless interior of the range—but those fish may have been hybridized out of existence by now, overtaken by the more domineering genetics of cutthroats and rainbows, those cospawners of spring. Packer and I have only explored a small fraction of the more than one thousand lakes in the Uintas, and we never caught a golden. As we grew up in Utah, the golden was something of a high-country legend. I remember hearing, reading, and thinking about the fish but never really considering how I might end up with one on the end of my line. As a youth, I never gave the golden trout more than a longing gaze as I turned the glossy page of some fly-fishing magazine and lost myself in some other salmonid or landscape that was seemingly just as far beyond my abilities and means.

All that changed one day in college while wandering the local bookstore. I chanced on Rich Osthoff's *Fly Fishing the Rocky Mountain Backcountry*. I flipped to the contents page and found a whole section devoted to my beloved Uintas. I bought the book immediately (even though my financial situation was just as dire as you might expect for a college student). I considered myself something a backcountry fisherman and thought this book might just polish off my skill set. Osthoff proved me naïve.

Here was a man who took the image of the casual backcountry fisherman and laughed in its face. He hiked alone—thirty, fifty, or seventy miles through wild country—camping among the boulders and sparse meadow grass of lakes perched nearly eleven thousand feet above the ocean. He dodged lightning. Stood tall and calm when bears entered his camp. Hitched his pack and walked twenty miles a day over trailless tundra at elevations too oxygen-deprived for trees to grow. He ditched his stove in favor of canned meat (*canned!*) because cooking noodles in the backcountry took too much time away from fishing and offered too little protein for his superhuman hiking plans. He even quit his day job when they wouldn't let him take the entire summer off to fish. Here was obsession, the refusal to compromise, the will to live with an eye only for one's goals. Here was a man unwilling to divorce himself from wildness. A man committed to more than driving to the edge of wild places and looking in. Osthoff immersed himself in the wildest places that the lower forty-eight had to offer—he swam deep into them like the trout he chased and only occasionally returned for civilized air. He was one step from a wild-eyed canyon hermit.

Like the golden trout (or the Yeti), Osthoff became a legend to me, a mythical figure roaming the backcountry and hitchhiking his way to trout towns and trailheads, always itching for high country and the next place full of trout that exploded the imagination. He was a man who made my devotion look like that of a weekend golfer. Never did I feel less serious about fly fishing and wild places than when I was drowning in the pages of Osthoff's book, following him on trails to backcountry lakes and streams of the Rocky Mountain West, just trying to keep up.

Osthoff's love for golden trout burns through the pages of his book. He loves them because they are rare and hard to find, because reaching the land of golden trout takes sweat and pain and even some luck. Because entering their world is not something that anyone with a free weekend and a credit card can accomplish. And most of all because they are achingly beautiful—a deep golden yellow splashed with brilliant red—and they live in lakes and streams just as rare and difficult and beautiful as the fish themselves. Seen through the lens of Osthoff, golden trout are the wilderness come alive, cruising the shoreline of a mountain lake miles off trail as a thunderhead crests a peak.

Lying in bed with the pages of that book lit up by the soft yellow of a desk lamp—my homework unfinished on the desk—I wanted to catch a golden trout very, very badly.

But whatever yearning I felt wasn't enough. Something happened when I clicked off the light. I did not want it enough to sacrifice the way I needed to—the way Osthoff did. I was too easily distracted. Life happened, as it tends to. I got married. I finished that homework and managed to graduate. Then we moved from Utah to Oregon. Suddenly I was farther from the Rockies and land of the golden trout than I had ever been. I left the backcountry to the truly dedicated and spent my fishing days on famous rivers and watching sea-run fish leap wildly as some prehistoric longing forced them up rivers and streams they knew as home. Osthoff's stories, though precious to me, ended up locked away in the attic of my mind, and my desire to catch a golden trout was up there with them, hidden in a mental steamer trunk.

So I got lazy and fat—figuratively and literally.

Besides occasional forays back to the Uintas with Packer—which were becoming rarer by the season—I began dining on easy-access fisheries. Big western rivers paralleled by roads and fisherman's trails that led from pullout to river and on to another pullout. These places are certainly wild in their own way, and I relished their mysterious intricacies—and their trout whose length and girth were just a fantasy in a Uinta lake. But such places, as fascinating as they were, took me farther away from the world Osthoff and his golden trout inhabited.

And the girth of those famous river fish was suddenly rivaled by my own. I began working in an office, stopped playing basketball, and lost the tall, lean shape that had made me a somewhat natural hiker. Suddenly I was bound by my own physical limitations as much as by location.

Eventually my wife and I moved again, this time to Idaho. I began volunteering with a Boy Scout group comprised of boys aged fourteen to eighteen. My days in the backcountry had started in such a company, and I was anxious to pass on something that might spark the love of wild places in those boys the same way that love had been sparked in me. We floated Idaho's Salmon River and climbed mountains. I saw young men who put the fourteen-year-old version of me to shame (and who left the thirty-year-old-version of me far behind). Somewhere along the way that golden trout in my brain picked the lock of that steamer trunk.

Each year our scout group planned a major trip, what we optimistically called our High Adventure. After a couple of years of rafting and mountain biking, that golden trout in my brain persuaded the whole group that we ought to spend a week backpacking in the Wind River Range of Western Wyoming—the major population center for golden trout in the Rocky Mountains. Many of the lakes and rivers in the Winds were stocked with golden trout (and other species) during the Great Depression by a local named Finis Mitchell. He wanted to start an outfitting company, but not enough of the mountain lakes had fish, so he yoked five-gallon buckets filled with water and fingerling trout across the backs of horses and mules and headed up the trail. He kept the water cool and oxygenated by covering the buckets with cold wet rags. It's the kind of bucket biology that would (rightfully) draw disapproving gasps given what we know now, but it worked out beautifully for Mitchell and the thousands of anglers who have since followed his lead into the Winds and fished for the wild offspring of those bucket minnows.

It helps that the Wind River Range has been protected by a trio of wilderness areas that were established over a twenty-year period from 1964 (when the Bridger Wilderness that protects the range's western slope was established) to 1984 (when the Popo Agie Wilderness was established). Between those two areas, the Fitzpatrick Wilderness was established in 1976—the year I was born. The three areas combine to include more than 726,000 acres, some 2,700 lakes, dozens of mountains that top out over 12,000 feet, and 54 glaciers—some of which are the largest remaining glaciers in the lower 48—all of which are receding due to climate change. It is a landscape that requires serious effort to access, but it offers a tremendous reward in return, for the moment at least. Thinking of the Wind Rivers in that way adds a new dimension to the name *golden trout*. The name seems especially apt when thought of as a reward for the effort it takes to catch one. But the golden trout of the Wind River Range don't have the monetary value their name connotes. They cannot be purchased in a traditional sense, and as a result they have not become a symbol of traditional wealth but rather a symbol of wildness. Because they reside primarily on public lands, they are an egalitarian treasure, available to a wide swath of the population. That is not to say there isn't a scarcity of golden trout. Just try to catch one.

Besides the history and geography of the place, the Wind Rivers had another draw: it was Rich Osthoff's favorite patch of land on the planet. His book made no secret of the fact that the Winds ought to be the destination of any serious golden trout angler. But before I could make it, I had to get serious again. I had to learn the price of gold. I started playing basketball three times a week. I started running stairs at the local high school football field. I cut down on the amount of deep fried food I was eating. My legs hurt, and my stomach ached. I tried thinking of a golden trout and kept running. When that didn't work, I imagined Osthoff calling me soft. I began losing my midsection. I started to gain a slight resemblance to the Uinta Mountains version of myself. I grew a beard. I loaded a pack with forty pounds of gear and began walking the neighborhood. Neighbors began to fear a homeless man was wandering their suburban streets, but I was trying to reduce the pain my shoulders would feel that first long day on the trail. One Saturday I hiked a trail along a small trout stream until I was miles from the trailhead. I stripped my overloaded pack from my back and rigged up a four-piece rod and fished. Casting straight up the narrow creek between bushy willow trees, I felt unhitched from civilization and suburbia. I felt something close to young again.

We targeted a base camp near several basins of lakes. The path we selected wound through some of the hardest, most unrepentant and beautiful country any of us had ever seen. Several lakes along the way were rumored to house the elusive golden. I managed to find room in my pack for a four-piece rod and a reel. Then I convinced a few of the older boys to go with me on some day trips that would take us to the land of the golden trout.

So we set out—four of us day-hiked six miles from camp (twelve miles round trip) up a thousand feet—to a lake that the guidebooks claimed held golden trout. We saw a moose and almost took the wrong trail (someone had apparently taken the junction sign as a souvenir), forded an icy river, and finally topped a rise near timberline to gaze down a gentle meadow slope at a beautiful mountain lake walled in by stone ridges on three sides.

As I rigged up, the mosquitoes swarmed in clouds and tried to carry me off. Before I got the line through the guides, I had put on long sleeves, a headnet, and a bucket of DEET. Finally, I looked through the mosquitoes and cast into the lake's outlet. Knowing that we were expected back at camp before dinner, I figured the outlet was the best chance to get a quick fish. And I was right. I caught a six-inch brook trout on the third cast.

My heart sank. Backcountry brookies tended to reproduce like rabbits in a closed pen, effectively overcrowding hundreds of lakes and streams. We had, in fact, spent the previous day catching eager brookies on nearly every cast in the creek that fronted our base camp. So I knew all about the brookies in these mountains. While they were beautiful fish, they were not golden trout.

I moved to the lake itself and caught a few more brookies where the outlet created enough of a current to drift a scud. Still no goldens. We moved up to the inlet end of the lake, and I caught still more brookies. Somehow, I couldn't be angry or even frustrated. Here we stood, at what felt like the top of the world, staring up at the walls inside a bowl of stone.

We hiked back to camp in time for dinner.

That night at camp I got out the map and a headlamp and considered one last shot. Seven miles from where we sat (and close to two thousand feet up), three lakes perched right at timberline. Three lakes that Osthoff had fished. All the research I'd done (which is something of a crapshoot with backcountry lakes) indicated these lakes held goldens. And there were some indications that the fish were pretty large.

Osthoff, I knew, would have made a meal of that trip. For him, a fourteen-mile day hike and nearly two thousand feet of elevation was a light breakfast. He had probably hiked ten or twelve miles in a single morning to reach those lakes, with a full pack on his back. And here I was, seven miles from the shoreline and waffling. Years earlier I had bought Osthoff's book and begun to dream of all the places he had put under his boots. That was the point that the golden trout had taken up a permanent if somewhat hidden residence in my gray matter. In less than two days we would be hiking out. I had no idea when—or even if—I might be back. Sitting by the campfire, I stared at the map and exhaled.

I knew then, as I know now, that I was not Osthoff. And that I never would be. I was destined to be something of a tourist in wild lands while Osthoff was a part-time resident on par with a marmot or a mountain goat. If I was trying to step in his boot prints, I was going to fail. I thought about the ache in my calf muscles, the dull pain in my right ankle. I thought about how stiff

I would feel after another night sleeping on the ground. And I realized that becoming Osthoff was not what mattered. It was the attempt that made the difference. Only by trying could I glimpse those geographies of hope that fueled the circuitous travels of all those like Osthoff—and those like Packer and my brothers and my father—who ventured to public lands in the hopes of communing with trout and wildness. My sense of belonging in such geographies, my sense of being a creature who feels even a little bit at home in such places, would remain ephemeral and incomplete if I spent the day in camp nursing my aches for the hike to the car. If I was going to feel pain, it ought to be in the pursuit of the golden, in the failed pursuit to live for a moment like a man who belongs in wild places rather than someone who drops by to visit.

The next morning, a small group of us got up early and departed while the rest of the camp slept. We were only three, having lost one boy to a bum knee. We strapped on our daypacks and headed up the trail, knowing that we were racing the ever-present possibility of afternoon lightning.

After a quarter mile, I realized I had forgotten my rod. So it was back down and up for me while the boys waited and chuckled about my ineptitude.

Four miles from camp we made the big climb, switchbacking up the side of a mountain where a small creek dove off a cliff. This feature ended any brook trout migration from the stream near camp. We climbed on. We hit the first lake, which rested at well over ten thousand feet, reflecting the bright sun of late morning. The outlet seemed devoid of fish, and I never saw a riser in the lake itself. The far end of the lake was fed by a waterfall-laden inlet.

So we climbed again, this time up an angled rock face where the trees dwindled and contorted in the altitude. Standing at the top of the shelf, the water dropped off behind us, and I stopped to take a photo. The boys hiked on and disappeared into a sparse stand of gnarled trees. As I put the camera back into its case, I heard a sound that was unmistakable—a sound that was the same here among the clouds as it was among the crowds of anglers on Silver Creek—the gulp of a trout's rise. I looked into the winding creek that linked the first and second lakes and saw a fish high up in the water. I could tell right away this was no six-inch brook trout.

I dropped everything and began to rig up my rod, shaking only a little. Eventually the boys made their way back down and got out their lunches, so they could eat and watch the show. They knew something of my pursuit. They were even rooting for me—probably so I would shut up about it.

Strangely (or perhaps fittingly), these backcountry fish were picky. They ignored the parachute Adams I tried first. As I fished, I began to pick out more fish in the clear water below me, so I switched to a small streamer and had one nip, but I missed the fish. Then I tried a small elk hair caddis and missed another strike. Then nothing for two dozen casts. Somehow I was screwing it up, all the effort and the work, the waiting and dreaming, the planning and scheming, the early start and the heavy climb, the retracing of steps for my almost-forgotten rod, years of reading and dreaming, months of jogging and running stairs, all for nothing because I couldn't hook a fish.

I moved upstream to a deeper hole. The boys, now bored, had decided to climb the mountain that shadowed the lake. As they prepared to go, I noticed a small stonefly fluttering overhead. Yes, a stonefly. It defied reason. I could never seem to time the hatch on the Henry's Fork, but here they were. I began to notice them flying in pairs and singles. So I knotted on a stimulator and made a cast above the heart of the pool where I could see several fish holding. As the fly curled around a current seam, a fish rose and inhaled it. I struck and came up solid.

I tried to cry out, but the sound caught in my throat and came out like a broken transmission. The boys looked over, saw the bent rod, and came running. It was a good fish for the backcountry—more than fourteen inches. It thrashed and jumped—oh how I wished I had my net and waders, which were only a few hundred miles away. Still, I managed to move the fish into the shallows and then reach down and lift it out of the stream. It was a beautiful fish, golden orange with a dark red splotch on the gill plate and brown spots down its side.

And two dark red cutthroat markings painted across the bottom of the jaw.

At first I didn't register the fact that it might not be a golden trout. I dismissed the cutthroat markings mentally, telling myself confidently (and irrationally) that this was normal. A voice in the back of my mind whispered that I had never actually seen a golden trout outside of those glossy magazine pages. That I didn't know what those markings might mean.

"It's a hybrid," I told myself and the boys, "but it's mostly a golden. It's more golden than cutthroat—look at the red splashes on the belly and gill-plate."

We high-fived like drunken idiots after I released the fish and the relief and satisfaction of accomplishing my goal was palpable, if perhaps inauthentic. I had almost convinced myself that the fish was a golden, that I had done it. I was ready to cross the golden trout off my list, even though I had only caught a hybrid. I was incapable of the honesty needed to confront my own failure.

And then—two casts later, as I tried to bask in the glow of it all, as I told myself I had finally done it, as the boys climbed that mountain—I actually did catch a golden trout, and I realized that first fish was mostly a cutthroat.

The second fish had a buttery yellow belly, a dark red mark on the gill plate, and a striking green tint to its back that had been missing from the first fish. It looked as if it had swum off a magazine page. Most importantly, it had no cutthroat markings, and it looked like no other fish I had ever seen in person.

I was forced to confront the fact that my initial prize had

been a cutthroat (probably a hybrid but likely more cutty than golden), and only my longing had turned the fish into a golden. Even in my moment of triumph, I proved to myself that I was no Osthoff. The idea that the Yeti-like Osthoff might climb up here (barely breathing hard) and convince himself that a cutthroat or a hybrid was an out-and-out golden, a descendant of a trout mule-carried and bucket-planted by Finis Mitchell, was crazy. But I nearly did that very thing. I was reshaping my memories to forget all about those cutthroat slashes. I was nothing more than a weekender, a pretender, a poseur in the wilderness. I didn't know wild places; I hadn't drunk them in like Osthoff. I was a just a tourist.

All these thoughts flashed through my consciousness as I gazed at that fish. And then I decided none of it mattered. Maybe I was reshaping memories again, but as I peered at the golden sides of that golden trout, I thought I could see something there—some sparkle of a type of wildness I thought I lost to the past. Since my days among the lakes of the Uintas, I had found a new type of wild place, the hidden yet clear wildness of wild trout streams—even those you can simply drive to. Those fish embodied a wildness that was different but no less valid. I had fallen hard for those streams and those fish and had thought I had to choose between the wild trout of rivers like the Madison and the Henry's Fork and the wild horizons of places like the Winds or the Uintas. But staring at that golden trout—at the destination of my wandering path to this place—I resolved to have both. I couldn't be Osthoff—not the pure strain badass that hiked seventy miles solo across grizzly country—but maybe I could be a slightly watered-down version, a hybrid not unlike that cutthroat I had mistaken for the genuine golden. I could fish famous blue-ribbon streams surrounded by fellow pretenders, and I could still occasionally wander among the granite cathedrals of mountain backcountry. If wildness comes in a variety of forms, I would try to sample all those available to me.

I released the golden trout. I stared at the granite and the choked green high-country grass, then peered through the water down to the fish finning near the bottom against the cobbled riverbed. I couldn't stop grinning.

I managed to catch half a dozen fish before we called it a day, and I even talked one of the boys through hooking and landing a heavy hybrid that went eighteen inches and really did look more golden than cutthroat. At some point, I looked up at the gray peaks that surrounded the basin and wondered why I hadn't come sooner. Why had I spent so many years fishing rivers paralleled by roads when places like this existed? A small part of me was eighteen years old again. I thought about Packer and the Uintas. I flashed back to a lake up a scree trail that I suddenly wanted to see. I stared at the high country that I loved but had forsaken.

Sure, after we hiked out of the Winds, it didn't take long for me to have my head turned. At the first rise of a good rainbow to a PMD on a famous tailwater, I momentarily forgot all about those places with stone peaks, wildflowers, and waterfalls. But I will always remember those fish—scarlet red on buttery yellow— and the cool breeze unique to the high country, the green and gray snowcapped world that exists more than a dozen miles from the nearest road and more than ten thousand feet up. And I will be back. I will seek out those places where entrance cannot be purchased by credit cards or handshake agreements, where the golden treasures are trout and the only currencies are sweat and willpower. The places where anyone can go but few actually do. The places where hope and golden trout wait for us all.

CONVERSATIONS WITH GRANDPA

"Henry Day used to take a bunch of us up to the lake in the early summer. We'd bring a half dozen boats and have a fish derby. Hen would usually win. If he fell behind he'd toss a handful of corn in the lake to chum 'em up. The limit then was twenty fish, and we'd fish from sunup 'til we took our limit. Fat trout. Not like those now. At night we'd go to the restaurant and the derby winner ate free. Hen Day fished in a big cowboy hat and he paid for the rooms. I knew him from Draper. This was before the Stump Ranch, before I learned steelhead. A handful of corn would turn it around for ol' Hen. He'd start catching trout right off the boat. We used worms, mostly. Hen's worms were tipped with corn."

"One time we walked down from the cabin and fished the evening. Your dad hooked a steelhead and it fought like a cornered wildcat. He reeled and reeled, walked up and down the sandbar. Finally his arms gave out and he handed me the rod. I reeled and paced. That fish never came topside, never jumped, just ran and fought. My arms were sore and I gave the rod back to your dad. We fought that fish for most of the evening, sure we had caught the record. A twenty-pound steelhead. We used to catch a fish almost every night. Right off the sandbar underneath the trolley line. That fish finally tired and we brought it in and it was a six-pound buck hooked in the tail."

"At midnight at the top of Middle Fork Peak, the stars were so close and so many, like a blanket made of heaven."

FIRST GOOD FISH

Like many anglers, I suppose, I can close my eyes at almost any moment and recall memories of trout. A hook-jawed brown in Montana that took a hopper with a satisfied pop, the lazy rise of a Henry's Fork rainbow sampling flav spinners, my first twenty-inch brown slowly approaching the surface to inhale a size twenty Griffith's gnat. These fish rise in the river of memory, sometimes at my call and sometimes at random moments, triggered by unclear stimuli. Either way, such memories are intermittent connections back to fish and the moments when those fish and I were connected. I try to remember all I can about the day, the river, the light filtering through the clouds or pounding down out of the blue, but the actual experience remains elusive, as if partitioned off by glass, even though the images might come easily. I think this is the reason we take so many pictures of fish—often holding them up like we are conquering heroes—so that sometime later, when trout and the places they inhabit are far from our reach, we can bring the memories flooding back like spring runoff and try to re-inhabit those moments. While such memories are imperfect, they do allow us—in some limited way—to keep fishing after we have left the river behind and ended up some place worth forgetting. I may not be able to relive those moments completely, but the effort to do so is often worth it.

When I flash back to a memorable fish, it is often a surface feeder. Right now, I can close my eyes and I can see the head-to-tail rise of a fish I have spent hours remembering—a seventeen-inch rainbow I caught in a fading dusk, the light tinged with red from ricocheting off the cliff faces in the canyon below Flaming Gorge Dam, when I was sixteen.

For years after the catch, this fish was without rival in my memory. Like many young people, I wanted to measure myself against the world, and a big trout seemed like a good ruler. Similarly, the Green River was a measuring stick of its own. It is still the trout stream that many Salt Lake City fly fishermen revere the most. It is a river quite unlike the freestone creeks and mountain lakes where I learned to catch trout. Below Flaming Gorge Dam, where John Wesley Powell floated before the dam existed, the river often flows through public lands and is especially accessible from a Forest Service trail that follows the stream through the steep, burned red canyon walls for seven miles. The Green, as we called it, was where I learned how little I knew. It is where I learned that seeing a fish did not mean catching a fish. Where I learned that I could not nymph fish very well, and that some trout prefer red-bellied humpies or rubber-legged terrestrials of various (real and imagined) denominations. Where I learned that fly fishing is a game with no end. It is endless searching and casting and confusion interspersed with occasional moments of perceived clarity. The Green is where I learned humility. I had learned none of that the night I took that first good fish. But I suppose that night was the one where I became hooked for good on fly fishing, the night I retired my spinning reel and my Mepps gold-blade spinners with the red dots.

I remember the evening light and shadows cast by the steep canyon walls. In a steep canyon, dusk arrives early and settles in for hours. Wall shadows collage the river, and in midsummer fish that have been sulking will begin to rise. It is a soft light, a pillow of dusk that cushions and blurs, making flies difficult to see and fish less edgy, more relaxed once the fence-rail sun of high noon is relaxed by the canyon shadow.

I was fishing an orange stimulator. And perhaps it was that night that led me to fish that fly so loyally for years afterward, even when it was not a great choice. I waded out as far out as I could, then I climbed onto a boulder and stood above the river and began to cast.

My brother Justin was fishing upstream, and (unbeknownst to me as I stood on the rock) he would catch three large trout that night on a cranefly larva. It was something of a milestone for both of us. For years we would talk about that night in reverent tones, though I don't know if he remembers it now. I don't know if that night is printed on his memory like it is on mine or if he tries to escape back into the waters of his past the way I sometimes do. The river currents braided and unbraided in tones of orange and green and steel blue. My stimulator drifted along a current seam for what felt like a hundred yards and an hour and a moment and then disappeared. In its place, a dark trout's head plunged back down into the river, replaced by a pink-striped silver side and a green back, which gave way to a tail, and then the fish was gone.

I set the hook and the rod throbbed and pulsed, the large trout curving my rod to an arch. The weight, the force of life, the line clicking off the reel as the trout ran toward the river's center—these were sensations I had not encountered before, and they startled me in their urgency, their wildness. Here was life, connected to me but not really under my control, the way a small trout is once hooked.

The fish in the Green are not natives, but they are wild. A native fish can trace its ancestry in a particular water back before the first fish hatchery. A wild fish must have been born in the water where it currently resides. Wild fish are sought after and considered superior to hatchery fish because they have attributes of wildness: they fight with more ferocity than hatchery fish, they feed and behave in ways that are more natural to their environment, and they grow large and fat and as colorful as a flag. In short, wild fish are at home in the river's ecosystem, while a hatchery trout is just visiting. Hatchery fish often end up dead within months of being released, never really adapting to the fact that they no longer live in a concrete feeding pen. A wild trout's pedigree jolts the angler alive the precise moment the fish is hooked, and the two are connected through nine feet of graphite, thirty yards of braided nylon coated with a vinyl shell, and nine or so feet of tippet-leader combination.

The fish's energy seems to shoot up this rig through the various knots and lines to the tip of the rod, down the length of the cork handle and into the angler's hands, where it is converted immediately into some kind of life-giving force that enters the bloodstream and occasionally (in the case of a large fish) elicits adrenaline and sometimes tattoos the fish onto the angler's memory. That force is spooky and defies traditional logic and doesn't seem to work for everyone, but when it does—when you find yourself connected to a good trout and you feel the elixir coursing—then you suddenly have an answer to the following question: How do I want to spend every second I can spare for the rest of my life?

The sheer number of wild fish in the Green River is astounding. There are fish everywhere, and you can see a host of them because the water is intensely clear. But hundreds more have melted into invisibility. You know they are there because this river is a wild trout sanctuary, and every cubic foot of water looks like a place a trout might live. Many anglers are tempted into fishing only for those fish they can see, which is still a large number. It is simply irresistible to fish to those trout in water so clear it might as well be a sliding glass door framing a nice view into the trout's backyard. In the years that followed that night on the rock I became quite good at fishing the Green's bankside eddies. The fish in many of those big clear-watered eddies are on display right off the Forest Service trail that runs parallel to the river below Flaming Gorge Dam. They are the trout most susceptible to anglers. Fishing for them is a thrill, picking out the trout that is finning a foot or two under the surface, the dark missile of a fish tipping up in slow motion to sip a speck of dust off the surface just often enough to keep you casting. Seeing that fish deliberately rise to your fly, poke its nose through the surface membrane, inhale the speck connected to your line, and begin to descend as you set the hook—it is an incredibly visual way to fish, and I was gut-hooked on it for a long time.

Eventually, however, I began to notice that these eddy trout fought with a distinct lack of hope. This is certainly anthropomorphism on my part, but it seemed like—being such a common target and having been caught before—these fish knew the story's end. They would thrash a bit and then allow themselves to be dragged in. They had decided that being caught was simply the cost of living in that particular river. As I learned how to fish the rest of the river (not just those trailside aquariums), I learned that a fish hooked at the bottom of a heavy run, or in any piece of water less accessible (or at least less fished), fought with zeal and energy that was distinctly wilder than its eddy-bound cohorts.

I like to tell myself that a wild fish hooked somehow transfers some of that wildness to the angler through the rigs and lines and knots. This is why wild fish are preferred over hatchery trout: because they have more wildness to give. I think these wild fish can regain that lost wildness given enough time and freedom and who really knows what else. But a fish that is fished over endlessly and caught three or four times a year (or more) loses some of what makes it wild in a way that it can never regain. It becomes somehow a *tame* wild fish—born and reared in a wild river but living in circumstances not altogether wild. Like a zoo animal or a pet wolf, such a fish is neither completely domesticated nor completely wild, inhabiting some state between the two that is not easily detected.

I hadn't thought of any of this when I hooked that first good fish, a fish that came from midriver rather than one of those trailside eddies. And I hadn't caught enough fish to know if it fought well. But I remember that sensation, the sheer force of life buzzing up the line like an electrical current and forcing its way into my heart—tying us together like a four-barrel nail knot. Even now I am still hooked to that fish in a way that is much more permanent than any trout I have hooked before or since. My first good fish measured exactly seventeen inches, nose to tail, and as I guided it back in the water it felt like a lightning bolt at rest, finning lightly in my hands beneath the glass surface until—with one powerful thrust—it disappeared into the dark blue of the night.

I caught one more fish before the light disappeared completely. That second trout was smaller, but beyond that I don't remember any details. Then I walked the river trail back to meet my father at the car, leaving my brother to fish alone in the dark.

I spent the whole walk—nearly a mile—trying to figure out what had just happened.

MISTRESS

"That river almost cost me my marriage."

This was a surprising admission. Standing in the hallway of a cubicle farm, the harsh white fluorescent lights ricocheting off the brown carpet walls, a man I had met maybe two or three times prior informed me rather offhandedly that an obscure local tailwater had nearly caused his marriage to end in divorce.

"It used to be a bottom release dam, you see." He looked past me and licked his lips, ran a suddenly nervous hand through his thinning hair. He was a chemist in his early fifties until this conversation turned. Now he was a fisherman. He knew that I was a fisherman, and I think he felt somehow compelled to continue.

"Before they reconfigured the dam, that river was unreal. I would drive down there after work every night during the summer and fall. Fish until midnight, throwing plugs in the dark. I couldn't stop. My wife, she wanted me to leave it, but I couldn't stop. Brown trout. That river . . ."

He trailed off. After a moment of silence, we went back to talking about the proposal that I was editing. When we shook hands at the end of the impromptu meeting, having agreed on a schedule for the proposal, his forehead sheened with sweat and his hand trembled. He gave me a toothy grin that creased his sun-hardened face.

"That river." He shook his head in dismay.

There are places that hook anglers as anglers hook fish. Just a few miles west of Yellowstone National Park, there is a large man-made reservoir. It is surrounded by a mix of national forest lands and private summer homes. On a map it looks like a three-fingered hand. Hebgen Lake. Every year the trout—having been conditioned by hatches and hatches of mayflies and midges—break the lake's surface in hunger, leaving evidentiary circles on the water that trout anglers call "riseforms." Riseforms break up a calm, glassy surface with an expanding ring of disturbance. Any August day the rings that dot Hebgen Lake's surface look like rows of scattered, heavy raindrops or the remnants of skipped stones, but the roots of those circles are trout, big trout. Such behavior is not normal for large trout in lakes. I have spent many days on Henry's Lake, just a few miles southwest of Hebgen, and seen only a handful of fish rise. And those Henry's fish were one-timers; they rose once out of some instinctual need to capture something that I—as a fisherman and not a fish—will never know. Then they returned to eating scuds and nymphs and other fish among the moss and aquatic vegetation near the lake's floor and forgot there was a transparent roof to their world.

I believe this is a product of behavioral conditioning. But I am not a biologist, so that is probably rubbish. Still, here is my theory: the fish in Henry's Lake rarely see enough bugs on the surface to give the surface more than a passing thought. There is no regular heavy callibaetis hatch on Henry's Lake in the summer. Hence, fish in Henry's Lake rarely look up, and when they do they are generally disappointed. But because bugs carpet the roof of Hebgen Lake more or less every day of the summer, the trout get used to all that food on the flat surface. They become accustomed to seeing and eating armadas of sailboat mayflies and midges struggling through the lake's surface membrane in an effort to be born while the flies born yesterday (those that survived) return to the surface and splay out for an egg-laying death—yes, Hebgen Lake trout eat both the newborns and the elderly. As my theory goes, these trout begin to think of the surface as a kind of bakery window. They can window-shop because (unlike the window at Henry's) there is often food on display—so they look up. Consequently, they are more likely to notice a morning hatch of mayflies or midges or a big caddis struggling against the sky of a warm summer evening. Every day of August those trout rise until the wind blows. And after a long winter, when May rolls around and midges start to congregate— big juicy chironomids—those trout remember the salad days of summer, and they rise. But next May you can go ten miles south to Henry's Lake and find similar numbers of midges perched on the lake's surface, drying their wings, preparing for flight. Their black-and-white segmented bodies are as thin as a pencil line but filled with enough protein to satisfy a trout that spent winter beneath the ice, or at least it would seem so. Still those Henry's Lake cutthroats won't rise. They don't look up. They stick to their own subsurface neighborhood.

Would it be different if Henry's got a big mayfly hatch every summer? I'd like to think so, but like I said, I am no biologist. It just seems right. All I know for sure is that those Hebgen Lake fish rise consistently. And I am gut-hooked by them. What my theory primarily reveals is that I have spent a lot of time—perhaps too much time—thinking about the trout that live in Hebgen Lake.

The fish in Hebgen are called gulpers. Their lips pop when they rise and the sound is a gulp and it sets my heart fluttering, kicks a tingling sensation down my spine and into my arms. I arrive in the August morning and the surface of the lake is a glassy tabletop. Callibaetis mayflies are lifting off postbirth or spinning in an egg-laying ritual predeath. The morning light glistens off the bugs as they flutter, illuminating them transparent and backlit. These insects are the harbingers of gulp. On the glass surface rings appear in the distance—to the west along the rocky shore of a bay, fish surface sporadically. Straight ahead fifty yards out, a fish rises every three or four feet, connecting the dots of mayflies, setting a course for shore, then correcting, circling, disappearing for five seconds and showing again in a rise that seems familiar, like the way you recognize an old friend by their gait. The black head shows dark against the white surface of dawn's rising sun. I blow hot air onto my hands and try not to panic in anticipation.

I pull my one-man boat off the roof of my car and push out into the water. Lines of force echo out beyond the air-filled pontoons like sonar, warning the trout of my arrival. I row out to the last place I saw a fish rise and I lower the anchor, taking care not to splash. I sit silent, lift a rod, pull the line, and find the end of the leader. I slip the needle-thin tip through the eye of a hook, then wet the last six inches of tippet so the knot won't brittle and snap. I wind together an improved clinch knot, an action that requires both my hands and my teeth, an action so familiar that I struggle to even describe it or think consciously about the steps required to tie it tight. My eyes do not leave the water for more than a microsecond. I finish with a three-way pull: the tippet in one hand, the tag end in my mouth, and the fly itself between two fingers. The knot slides up the translucent leader until it snugs against the round eye of a size fourteen gray parachute spinner. My fingers grab the nippers on my vest, and I clip the tag of line created by the knot, leaving a tight, three-barreled junction between the fly and the tippet. I look away from the water only long enough to ensure I don't inadvertently clip my fly into the lake. Then I pull enough line off the reel to cast and coil it on my stripping apron, my boat's green pontoons still on the glassy surface. I try not to move, try not to breathe, try not to talk to myself, try not to think too loudly. I become stillness itself and watch the flat lake's top for signs of trout.

A black head chased by a dorsal fin breaks the surface thirty yards to my right, then rises again, farther out, on a path that won't lead into my somewhat limited casting range. I do not lift the anchor and give chase. *I will not chase fish. I will not chase fish. I will not chase fish.* I repeat the mantra, knowing that chasing trout on this lake is a version of three-card monte. As soon as I vacate, a good trout will rise where I just left. No, it is better to wait. A fish will rise close, and I will have a chance, if I wait. So I do. And a fish surfaces to my left, twenty yards away.

I lift the rod and false cast, shooting line off my apron and into the air, lengthening and lifting so I can fire it toward the diminishing specter of the fish's last meal, guessing which way the fish will go next. I shoot the fly out to the right of the riseform, and it lands somewhat haphazardly, the fire-orange parachute post catching the sun's rays for a moment, but the fish rises again on a different course, coming at me now. My fly has overshot that path, and I pick up in a panic, pulling the fly off the surface in a rush, disturbing the water. I have too much line out. I strip furiously, trying to adjust in midair to this new closer target when the trout rises again, closer still, and I stop my cast midstroke, the fly dropping to the surface like a dry leaf on a light breeze still two feet beyond the last riseform. The fish never shows again, probably spooked by the boat or the boat's captain and his frantic flails.

I wait. A fish rises out in front of me but too far. Then it rises again, on a line that won't bring it to me. *I will not chase fish. I will not.*

Can fish obsess over something? Probably not. But if they could, I would bet that Hebgen trout are obsessed with surface feeding. They wander and pace, searching for their next fix. They seem to be addicts. But they have brains the size of a tablespoon. So obsession seems like a reach because it probably involves emotion and conscious thought. Obsession is best left to humans, especially those of us who fly fish for trout.

Generally speaking, I favor a balanced life—even if I don't always live one. I think it is sometimes wise not to fall too deeply in love. I love to fish for trout, especially with dry flies and especially for large trout that are rising metronomically to a good hatch of mayflies or caddis. I tend to think about these trout often and in complex ways that sometimes surprise me.

Sitting in the florescence of a conference room, my face lit by PowerPoint, I find myself wondering about water temperature and bugs and river flows and barometric pressure. I think about the migration patterns of salmonflies and the mating behavior of gray drakes, the life cycle of bugs whose Latin species names I have taught myself to pronounce. I can close my mind at this moment and picture a run on the Henry's Fork that I am dying to fish again soon. And I can tell you the very day next spring when I am likely to be back at that place. I love trout fishing, perhaps more than I should. I am not obsessed, but I am not that far off. I worry about this.

I am not referring to obsessive compulsive disorder or other difficulties that plague so many against their will. No, I am talking about wanting to fish so much and so badly that I begin to lose perspective about the rest of my life. That is what I worry about. Because here's the thing about the kind of obsession I am talking about: it is inherently selfish. To be obsessed in this way is to willfully ignore anyone's needs but your own. Willfully, as in you choose to be a jerk. Assuming you are a mentally healthy human, if you pursue obsession and spend every waking hour of every day thinking about the object of your desire, you are at the same time choosing not to think about the needs and desires of those around you—including those you profess to love. This is not good human behavior. They don't tell you that in the glossy full-spread advertisements of fly-fishing magazines; it doesn't make for a catchy slogan.

I have a wife and two daughters. To say that my forays to trout waters do not affect them would be a lie. They spend nights alone while I camp on trout streams or drive home in the dark. My girls wish Dad would spend a few more summer afternoons playing soccer or going to the local swimming pool. My wife wishes I spent less money on obscure fly-tying materials and less time surfing the internet for used drift boats. I wish these things as well; at least part of me does. The part that isn't thinking right now about Hebgen Lake and the gulpers there. The part that doesn't spend every winter checking the air temperatures and fishing reports in New Zealand and Patagonia.

The part of me that sometimes wishes he was less afflicted is a church-going, happily married father of two and a nine-to-five resident of Cubicle City. This man worries too much about his kids. He worries about his parents, who are getting older. He loves his wife fiercely. He plants tomatoes and corn and mows the lawn on Saturdays (even though he deplores mowing the lawn). He shovels the walks in the winter and helps his neighbors move. He coaches soccer when he doesn't have to work late. He shoots the bull with neighbors and tries not to engage in conversations about politics if at all possible. He knows that his passion for fly fishing is not always easy on his family or his wallet. He knows his addiction to fishing is something his neighbors shake their heads at or laugh about nervously or use as a measuring stick for their own radicalism: "At least I'm not like Grover. At least I know my limits."

But there is another part of me that can spend the next hours or minutes (is there a difference?) picturing the glassy surface of Hebgen Lake or a tailout of a Henry's Fork riffle and envision the heads of trout rising to mayflies and caddis, the man who longs for New Zealand and goes fishing at least every other Friday and spends much of his day dreaming of rivers and lakes and the trout that swim therein. This trout-sick man is not rich. He plays the Monopoly game at McDonald's, dreaming of trout camps in Alaska and Argentina. He knows that being wealthy would increase his chances of seeing a New Zealand summer. He is a man who loves fly fishing for trout perhaps a little more than he should.

These two men—the soccer dad and the trout-sick fly angler—have generally struck an uneasy truce inside of me. I would be naïve to think that incredible, important, and beautiful things don't happen away from the river. The problem is that one must leave the river occasionally to figure out what those things are. I have been more nervous and happy watching my daughters play soccer than I have been fishing the green drakes on the ranch, but I had to skip fishing that day to figure that out. Sure, the perfect compromise is to take your kids and your wife fishing. And I do. My family doesn't simply tolerate my angling; they embrace it. My wife often implores me to go fishing because she knows it makes me happy, and she wants me to be happy. My kids want to see pictures and talk about places I have been. We talk about how old they have to be before they can wade the Henry's Fork.

But there is a big world out there, and my girls want to experience some portions of it that are not home to rising trout. So we do. It is not a matter of bearing the burdens of such times—it is admitting to myself that happiness exists away from trout water as well as knee-deep in it. This need to fish isn't all consuming, or it doesn't have to be, at least not for me, even if there was a time when I thought it should be. Even if the marketing departments of major fly-fishing brands are trying desperately to convince me that I must fish more, harder, longer, for more elusive fish in more remote places with more expensive rods.

Those who make their living selling fly-fishing gear have a tough job. Many in the industry remember the uptick that came with the movie *A River Runs through It*. People started fishing, things started selling. That, of course, did not last. Current reports from the industry range in tone from near panic to steely determination. Some years ago, the fly-fishing industry started releasing the equivalent of Warren Miller ski films. These movies don't have the commercial power of *A River Runs through It*, but they do espouse a certain ethos. They paint their heroes as uncompromising fishing pilgrims on the road to enlightenment. These young men (and lately women have started to show up as well) have a singular goal: catch big fish. Often those fish are caught in places that required long jeep rides or floatplane landings.

The twenty-two-year-olds in the films do what they had to do to get to such places. I admire that. They are living their dreams.

However, the culture of fly fishing has decided in some way that this should be a shared dream, a communal dream we are all having together. A troutbum's life has become the life one aspires to. Drop everything and go fishing. You don't need anything else. The river is life. The riseform is its manifestation. If you want to know it well, you'll need this seven-hundred-dollar rod.

I don't begrudge anyone that life. I wanted it for myself once. Until I didn't. I realized that I wanted two lives: the soccer dad and the fisherman. When I fish, I fish hard. From dawn till dusk (or beyond), every other Friday. Weekends in the spring, a week in the late summer, every October day I can spare. Packer and I once fished sixteen hours in a row with only occasional stops for urination, granola bars, water, and beef jerky. I want to cast farther. I want to tie better flies, understand rivers and trout more than I do now. I want to catch steelhead and bonefish and permit. But I am not willing to end up with a shaky hand and a look in my eye that says I can't control it. Ishmael said of Ahab: "He seemed ready to sacrifice all mortal interests to that one passion" (1967, 182). I don't want to say: "That river nearly cost me my marriage."

But I do understand how a person could end up in that place. For me, that place would be Hebgen Lake.

The sacrifice of one's life in the pursuit of one's passion neatly exemplifies the dangers of viewing public lands and wilderness as a place to escape from civilization. Escape itself is a kind of drug, a fix that—for all of its potential indirect benefits of recharging the batteries and providing perspective—doesn't provide any direct benefit to whatever a person is attempting to escape *from*. When wilderness is only a means of escape, the ills of civilization are rarely remedied. Instead, they are forgotten or left behind for those who cannot or choose not to escape, including those who profit from the ills of civilization. When the escapee returns from the wilderness, the problems haven't worked themselves out. Often they have gotten worse, and the call of wilderness escape becomes all the more alluring while the potential indirect benefits continue to shrink.

The literature of Western civilization is filled with stories in which the natural world is an escape from the civilized, industrialized setting where a person's problems just won't give them a break. Those who study stories for a living call this kind of story—in which a person attempts to escape civilization for the simple life of nature—a "pastoral." As you might suspect, the word pastoral is linked with agriculture (particularly shepherds). It's also perhaps unsurprising then that the American West—the place where all these public lands are located—is the setting for the largest pastoral story in American history. Settlers came west, we are told, to strike out on their own, to free themselves from industrial eastern cities and find the garden of the world, the land of milk and honey. So what are we to make of the West today, a place in which civilization is omnipresent with massive cities such as Phoenix and Los Angeles and the infrastructure systems needed to prop them up in a warming climate and a shrinking supply of water? What are we to make of the fact that America's pastoral story led to environmental disasters like the 1930s Dust Bowl and has choked off one of the region's primary arteries—the Colorado River—so that it no longer reaches the sea? Did escaping civilization work out for us? What happened to the garden?

It seems to me that our relationship with wild landscapes cannot only be one of escape because escape is an illusion. Taken to extremes, escape is the kind of thing that wrecks marriages. Rather, we have to realize that those cities and their inhabitants contain their own kind of wildness, one that isn't always healthy but generally remains hidden. We have to learn how to preserve a healthy wildness in our cities rather than making wildness invisible in them. Similarly, public lands serve as a series of corridors in which humanity and wild nature can coexist. Many public lands already do this; they offer us our best chance.

Last year I fished Hebgen Lake with Packer. We arrived at midnight and erected the tent, climbed in, and passed into a black sleep. Our lives complicated our fishing. The two men who battle inside of me wage a similar competition inside of Packer, but his fisherman loses more often. Life limits our chances to fish the way we would like. So we are reduced to arriving at midnight.

The gray and misty morning light woke us. We crawled into the crisp predawn of Montana's August. We readied and launched our boats, then kicked and rowed toward a couple of elusive risers. The wind stayed calm, but the fish were inconsistent. Several hours later I found a good pod of risers and anchored at the edge of them, determined to make a stand.

The fish circled and rose, their feeding sounds filling the heavy morning air, interspersed with only the occasional mechanical moan of a ski boat or the shriek of a fallen skier. The trout rose in ellipses and figure eights or patterns too intricate to determine by connecting the dotted riseforms but evident enough to make my mantra easy. *I will not chase fish.* And I didn't have to. One or two refrains and there was another target. I pivoted the boat to the left and fired. The trout were gulping now, rising every foot or eight inches, creating a dotted line like the cutout directions on my daughter's homework. My casts fell between riseforms, mistimed or mismatched. I changed flies; I cast again. A fish rose two inches to the left of my fly and I set the hook out of instinct. More rises, more rings. Gulping sounds surrounded me like frogs in a night swamp. I focused on one fish coming into range, rising deliberately, taking a wandering path from bug to bug to—finally—my fly, which it ate using the same riseform, the same economical movement, it had used to eat the naturals.

I leaned back into the fish, raising the rod, water spraying from the line as it went tight in the air—my back and arms triangled between the surface and the line, the fish thrashing in the triangle's point. The trout jumped then ran at the boat. I stripped line fast and turned the craft as the trout missiled out behind me. A minute later I dipped my net and scooped the fat rainbow up.

After a measurement and a release, I checked my watch. I had been fishing for six hours. This was not my first trout of the day, but I was still in single digits. Just a handful of fish, yet six hours had passed like a lunch break. I could barely remember anything except the riseforms—those semicircles and dotted lines—and the moment of the last take. This fishing was intoxicating. I realized suddenly that I really needed to pee.

A ONE-SIDED CONVERSATION WITH A BROWN TROUT

It was brown drake season and a smattering of the big bugs had been hovering over the water all day, just enough to stir the trout and excite the anglers, but never enough to launch an event of significance. Things started well. I fooled a brown trout with a drake in a narrow, fast chute of water just after my father and I climbed the pyramid of stairs that straddled the wooden fence and waded knee-deep through corn-colored meadow grass and wild wheat to this open stretch of water. The fish took the fly in a spurt of water and thrashed the surface, running to the far bank before surrendering onto its side, showing deep red spots amid the honeys and yellows and browns of its exterior.

But that was hours ago. Since then I had caught only a few small fish. The rises were intermittent, as if the fish and bugs could never quite agree on just what was happening. The sun was up high and the sky was that brilliant hue of western blue that comes from dry air and no smog. We were waiting for the evening spinner fall, hoping the swarm of bugs ritually circling the river would fall in an egg-laying splendor and those big chocolate mayflies splayed dead across the water's surface would stir the river's large resident brown trout to action.

As we waited a snout popped up now and then, against the far bank, across a wide, shallow stretch of water that glided over gravel and sand and moss and mirrored back the blue of the sky and the occasional white cloud. The fish was tucked in among the standing grass of a meadow bank and the current swirled just enough to complicate the drift. The trout rose so close to the bank that the riseform was rendered a half moon. I sat in the tall grass and watched. The snout was at the far end of my casting range, and I feared that stepping into the river would send shockwaves across the surface and spook it. A mix of small caddis and brown drakes that seemed almost the size of hummingbirds droned and hovered over the bankside weeds. Upriver a small trout or two rose occasionally in an eddy, splashing after the massive drakes. But across the river, that snout pocked the surface just often enough to keep me looking across always.

Finally, some cloud cover dulled the sun and the trout rose three times in a minute—three half circles in the edge of the watercress. I hunched low in the weeds and peeled line off my reel—the sound clicking in the afternoon silence. I leaned back into the cast, hauled the line, and shot the size ten parachute drake over the flat mirrored surface until it hit the end of the string and dropped like a snowflake, caught the wrong current, and began to drag as it rode past the fish.

I let it float downstream and then pulled the fly back to me. The fish rose again, not yet spooked. I stripped in and blew droplets of mist off the hackle points. The trout rose again. I looked at the water off the bank just in front me and thought about the caddis mixed in with the drakes milling around the streamside grass. I looked downstream at my father, casting long loops across the river. The trout rose again. I fished my caddis box out of my vest pocket and picked out a size sixteen improved X-caddis. The trout rose again. I knotted on the fly and began to false cast.

The trout rose again.

I cast poorly, came up short. Cast again longer but clumsy and hard.

The water was still.

Half a minute. One minute. Longer.

I began to cast again out of habit and anger; I was sure I had spooked the fish. But then the snout broke the surface a yard upstream from the previous spot. I tried to change the target in mid-cast and just pulled it off, the fly landing a moment's drift above the fish and floating lucky through the window, my breath halted, my voice a whisper:

"Eat, fish. Eat."

But no rise came, no half moon expanding, no snout. The fly drifted a foot past. Eighteen inches. And then I lost sight of it as it edged toward the far bank in the reflections and the shadows, and something in me said, *Strike!*

So I raised the rod, unsure but hopeful.

And the line came tight, electric, alive.

THE BIG V

On a favorite river, Packer and I took to naming water. Pools, runs, riffles—anywhere that consistently gave up fish got a name. In one stretch of fast water, a large boulder split the current. Trout lived in the shelter behind that rock, safe from the heavy current and happy to sample any food that drifted by. We gave it a rather unimaginative name: the Big V.

The first year we fished it, the V gave up some excellent fish, though we didn't land many of them. Because of the fast water just below, some slick rocks that made for precarious wading, the overhanging willow tree at the end of the run, and the discarded wooden door that was lodged between two midriver boulders just downstream, any fish that bolted down river was a good bet to break off or come unbuttoned. Once, just a few minutes after landing the largest fish I had ever taken from the hole, I hooked an even larger fish. I avoided all the dangers, only to have the fish come off as we tried to net it.

The following winter, as I came upon the Big V, I wondered if it would still hold fish in this frozen season or if they would seek deeper, slower water. I fished it in the morning on my way downstream to somewhere else and hooked nothing. On the way back to the car, I couldn't help but take another shot. On the second cast my indicator dipped and I set. The rainbow submarined out of the V, past my feet, around the willow, inside (through?) the wooden door and into the eddy below.

As I tried to work my way out of the fast current without breaking my rod or my ankle or falling in the river, the fish thrashed twice on the surface two holes down, and spit the fly.

That was the last fish I have hooked in the Big V. The V itself still exists and looks similar enough, though the water upstream and down has changed and the door has moved on to mark some yet undiscovered entrance down river. But the river channel has changed in ways I can sense but cannot see. Something hidden there under that broken surface is different in some fundamental way that eludes me—different enough to displace all those fish that used to call the place home or perhaps different enough to change the way my fly drifts through that slot, somehow exposing my fly for the fraud that it is. Either way, fishing the run has become a fruitless endeavor.

There is something lonesome about losing a place you once counted on. Sure, I'd rather lose good water to a changing river than to something else, like a private property sign or an environmental screw up. But lost water forces an angler to confront the reality that nothing is static, that these places we love are changing just like those places we have come here to escape. We like to imagine nature as a place untouched by humanity, this monolithic bastion of unchanging truth that will expose all the lies of civilization if we can just tap into its eternal, unchanging truths. But nature is always changing—often so slowly as to be invisible to our human impatience but sometimes quicker than we would like. In 1959 a Montana earthquake sent the side of a mountain into the valley below, dammed the Madison River, flooded the river valley to create a new lake (with the comparably unimaginative but infinitely more apt name Earthquake Lake), nearly destroyed the dam at Hebgen Lake, and killed twenty-eight people.

In his poem "The Beautiful Changes," Richard Wilbur writes about nature changing in "kind ways" and how such changes lead to "second findings." He writes that our previous knowledge of such places is replaced by "wonder" (1963, 226). Nothing is more beautiful to me than a trout river, and perhaps nothing changes more. Each drop of water, each cubic foot, each current seam slowly bends the landscape to its will—the loose dirt and gravel, midstream boulders, the mountainside, even the stubborn stone walls of a canyon are being slowly polished away. In a kind of irony, water is nature's primary agent of change in the arid West, though the schedule is kept with a geologic clock. Change comes first in ways that we cannot see but can sometimes feel. The most we can hope for is that our rivers change in "kind ways."

Perhaps more importantly we must learn to relish those "second findings" of a stream we once knew well. A changed river is a new river. There are new challenges, new lessons to learn, and new mysteries in that blue-green deep where the current drops off a newly formed gravel bar. There is that sweet surprise when you feel a head shake and lift that first fish from the water of a place you know you will return to, until the new place is also swallowed up, rewritten by water, reborn, and lost "back to wonder."

The Big V's constant change also reminds me of the fallacy of a static existence. Because the physical world we inhabit is always changing—be it a trout river or a mountain range or a city block—we must let go of the idea that standing still or capturing some version of the world in its prehuman state is even possible; we can't keep landscapes from changing. Certainly no landscape of the American West has been static, simply waiting for humanity to arrive. Change on a geologic clock is still change, and it is—as Wilbur writes—often a beautiful change. But change can also be brutal and violent. Humanity's track record is not so much one of "spoiling" virgin landscapes but one of accelerating and altering the process of change that is constantly taking place.

Humanity also offers its own version of "second findings": landscapes that have been nursed from illness to health. The Elwha River in Washington is one such example. When the largest dam removal project in U.S. history managed to do away with the Elwha Dam, salmon reentered the upper Elwha for the first time in nearly a century and the river's ecosystem rebounded as the river brought a fresh batch of wood and sediment to the estuary where the river enters the ocean. This material had been missing from a system that needed it. The wood and sediment benefited herring and smelt, which in turn benefited killer whales and bird life. Certainly the new Elwha is not the same river it was the day before dam construction began, but that river is an arbitrary and impossible goal: it only lasted a day, it was always changing. Instead, we should be looking for a healthy river.

Public lands can't offer a version of what life here was like before people. Rather, they can offer a window into what life can be like when people care for the land. Healthy public lands are a model for how we can live with a landscape rather than against it.

PART THREE

RENEWAL

THE STUMP RANCH FISH

We had an old gray Ford van. Not a minivan but a full-size passenger van, except my father had removed the third seat so he could put a dirt bike in the back. It was that kind of van. The color was a literal primer gray—no final coat of paint, just the primer.

When we would drive to the Stump Ranch, Dad would lay down an old mattress in the back. The mattress was sort of a puke yellow spotted with drawings of red dogs. The night before we left, he would load the van, surrounding the mattress with knapsacks full of clothes and a Coleman cooler. The next morning, he would wake his four children in the blackness of 4:00 a.m. We would stumble out to the van, throw open the sliding door, pile into the backseat, and try to go back to sleep. My sister would take the first shift on the mattress. Dad would ease the van out of the driveway and head north.

During that first hour of travel I often tracked the sky from my window, watching it go from black to deep blue until finally a dawn-blue gradient would force its way over the mountain horizon. The fireball sun would crest the Wasatch peaks, providing enough light that I could begin reading whatever Stephen King paperback I had stashed in among the gorp and beef jerky.

Around the time we got to Ogden, Dad would dig a box of eight-track cassettes out from under his seat, and we would listen to sixties surf rock and Simon and Garfunkel. Eventually, the August sun would begin to cook the inside of the van, and we would crack the windows. When we reached Salmon—eight hours later—we might stop for ice cream.

They called it the Stump Ranch because many of the trees at the front of the property had been cleared, leaving only the stumps. This was standard practice when Anglo-American settlers came west—clear the land, leave the stumps. There are probably hundreds of Stump Ranches across the Rockies that pay homage to the Homestead Act.

In an interesting way, this patch of land is an important part of the debate over public lands, even though it couldn't be more private. There are those who would like to see a twenty-first-century version of the Homestead Act in which western states sell their public lands to the highest bidder. Some of these same people would like the federal government to transfer some (or all) of its many acres of public lands to the states to aid in the process. Most Americans think this is a terrible idea. Land deeded to nineteenth-century settlers who made the many Stump Ranches across the West was given away because the American public thought that was the best thing it could do for the country as a whole. Much of today's rhetoric around public lands focuses on how land sales would benefit the local community, individual ranchers, or corporate energy companies, while the will of the nation as a whole is ignored. It is unclear if selling off public lands would help local communities. Plenty of people—including me—believe that public lands can be a useful asset for local economies. One thing we know for sure is that the American public—you know, the landowners—are strictly in favor of keeping public lands in public hands. A 2014 poll of western states found that 74 percent of western voters are against selling public lands (Colorado College 2014).

Some in the West talk about public lands as if the federal government took them away from the states and ought to give them back, but the truth is that the land has belonged to the federal government since it was acquired by the nation, before which it belonged to indigenous populations for a millennia we sometimes forget. Much of the Southwest was purchased in a bloody war with Mexico (an event that can accurately be called a land grab) in which American soldiers from across the country fought and died. Homesteaders bought their land from the government with sweat and perseverance or eastern capital betting on western resources. So each Stump Ranch that was settled as part of the Homestead Act should be treasured because it represents sacrifices from more groups than one, and because public lands are a material reminder that we exist as a nation and that the nation exists as a network of histories and geographies rather than some grand narrative. Public lands tie the various versions of America together through our joint ownership. Such links shouldn't be scoffed at. This particular Stump Ranch linked my family together in important ways throughout my childhood and—in my mind—it still serves as a link to my grandfather, who died years ago and sold the Stump Ranch before he went.

Seeing what used to be my grandpa's place now, you wouldn't get any idea that it was ever called the Stump Ranch. Now, Boy Scouts from Idaho, Montana, Utah, and Washington camp on the hillside where my brothers and I dodged sagebrush and played baseball with rocks and sticks. They call it a High Adventure Base, but the word "adventure" seems like a misnomer. The whole place seems less wild to me now than it did then. Sure, they float the river and they climb the rocks behind the old cabin. But it all feels as if the land itself has given up, resigned to whatever fate humanity has in store for it. When I was a kid, it felt like that mountain country had reached some sort of uneasy truce with my grandfather, a peace that could be lost at any moment with a single miscue from either side.

Grandpa bought the land from a midwestern couple. He got a good price because the river split the land from the road—there was no good way to access the property. At some point, someone had built a small one-room cabin about halfway up the hill, then gave up on making the place habitable.

This was the lesson my grandfather taught my father: you can make anything work, even if you have no idea how.

Grandpa was a builder. Things started in his imagination and he willed them into existence. In 1963, when my father was twenty-three years old, he and Grandpa built a wildfire lookout on the top of Middle Fork Peak, overlooking the Middle Fork of the Salmon River and some of the wildest, least disturbed public land in the lower forty-eight states. The lookout is still there, perched on the rocky top of a mountain like a hawk ready to take flight. They worked all summer and into the fall until the snow forced them out of the high country.

The road to the lookout ends fifty yards or so from the structure itself because the mountain steeps heavily at the last. The trickiest part of the build was getting the materials up that last incline. My grandfather solved this problem with a pile of lumber, a long cable, and his Studebaker pickup. They mixed the cement at the bottom of the hill, then pulleyed the batches to the top in a barrow. Grandpa could see solutions instead of problems. And he didn't let a lack of experience deter him. When they laid the brick for the lookout, my father was impressed that his dad could do the job so well.

"Where did you learn to lay brick?" he asked his father.

"Right here," the old man said without stopping.

On those summer evenings, the stars and the mountain air carried radio waves of Vin Scully's tenor all the way from California. The signal came in best when the Dodgers were playing a night game. Sandy Koufax and Don Drysdale led the team to the series where they beat the Yankees. Dad and Grandpa would sit on the top of that mountain and listen to baseball. When he was older, my father talked about those nights as if they were the moments when he came to actually know his father, in a place where they could begin to understand one another. Curtained by a sky washed with stars, Vin Scully's voice riding the night air, and a mountain beneath them, pushing them heavenward, they talked and laughed and listened to each other. Something happened on top of that mountain that made my father understand his father, something that drew us all back to the Stump Ranch each August.

They built the trolley at the Stump Ranch with the same spirit they used for the lookout and a cable as thick as my twelve-year-old wrist. They snaked the cable across the river as tight as they could get it and wrapped it around a boulder the size of a small car. Then, as if this was the kind of thing happening in suburban garages across America, they built a trolley car.

The seat of the car was a terrifyingly thin piece of plywood bolted into a metal frame that Grandpa dreamed up and talked a friend into welding together. He welded in handholds by the trolley wheels, but there were no guard rails on the sides. Passengers were advised to sit in the middle.

When we arrived at the cabin, my dad would honk the van's horn and we would pile out and stretch, looking down the steep slope between the road and the river. Gazing across the water, we could follow the trail my grandfather's boots had worn into the brown grass and dirt up the hill from the river to the cabin. The cabin door would open, and out would come Grandpa in a cowboy hat and a flannel shirt. It didn't matter that it was one hundred degrees and climbing. Grandpa wore flannel. He would wave and start down the hill toward the trolley platform. Once he boarded and shoved off, the cable would hum and moan like a drunk violin. Down the slope to the middle of the river the note would hold steady—one long groan. Then, once he hit the middle and started on the upslope, the cable sounds became a series of violent coughs timed with each great jerk as he dragged the car up to civilization. My grandfather had massive hands. He would wrap them around the cable between the trolley wheels and pull. The car lurched forward as if it had been kicked from behind.

Once he had landed, we would stack some gear onto the plywood, then five or six of us would climb onto the trolley car, which seemed to me as if it could only safely hold four. My mother, sitting at the back, would unhitch the chain that anchored the car to the earth and we would roll out away from solid ground, above the river, speeding the downslope toward the far bank.

The river crossing took place high over the green water. Looking down was generally a poor choice. The car raced a blur down the slope of the fat cable to the middle, where it would pace back and die if not pulled up the other side by my father's own calloused hands. Unable to help myself, halfway across, I would look down at the water and then squeeze my sister till she couldn't breathe. I was sure that I was going to fall off that trolley car; it was only a question of when. Only when the platform appeared below would I remember to breathe.

Grandpa turned eighty when I was a boy, but he could still pull himself across the river on a piece of plywood. To my twelve-year-old mind he was simply too strong to ever die. He used that oversized pulley to connect himself to his neighbors and the world of pavement, as a transport between the world of mountains and the world of roads. It was the way he went across when he wanted to buy groceries or tools or a new fly rod. It was the way they hauled lumber and bags of cement across to build the cabin. They even took a jeep across the river using the trolley, a system of come-alongs, and a healthy dose of confidence. The old jeep was dying a rusty death in the sagebrush near the cabin when I last visited.

Once we were across we had free run of the place. The cabin was nestled into a draw where the mountains steeped and climbed, flanked by a ridge of black rocks forming a cliff. In the heart of the draw, a finger of water danced its way back and forth down the mountain from a spring near the top of the ridge. My grandfather had installed a series of pipes from the spring to carry the water down the hill, using one thousand feet of gravity to create water pressure for the cabin's indoor plumbing and the sprinkler system. In front of the cabin he had a patch of grass and a cadre of giant rain birds throwing arcs of spring water that stung my siblings and I like drops of ice on August afternoons. That same water nursed the wild raspberry patch that twisted and blossomed on the south corner of the property.

One year, rattlesnakes got into the raspberries, and we were told to stay near the cabin as Grandpa and Dad soldiered down the trail armed with shovels. They returned with a bucket of fresh red berries and bloody shovel blades. Grandma Tommie turned the raspberries into jam. She baked rolls and pies, cooked whatever meat we trolleyed across the river, and played gin rummy with my mom in the afternoon.

Sometimes the water from the tap would go brown. This was a sign that a bear was in the spring—drinking, playing, bathing, whatever bears do with fresh water. Once the water cleared, Dad and Grandpa might take us up the humid, leafy trail to visit the spring and make sure the pipes were okay. Sometimes, a fresh bear print was pressed in the mud, water collecting in the palm. Dad liked to stamp his own boot print right over the top of the bear's track. Back then it scared me. What if the bear comes back and gets mad? I thought. But now it seems fitting. This was the bear's place, but it was our place as well. A shared territory—wild and tame like the spring water in the pipes, the wild raspberries cooled by sprinklers in the heat of summer, the untamed river straddled by a contraption of cable, wood, metal, and willpower. A borderland between wildness and civilization, the closest thing he could find to a frontier, this was my grandfather's home.

Now, the High Adventure Base has replaced the old trolley car with a fancy all-metal car that holds six or seven Scouts easily and has high side rails and benches to keep anyone from falling out. But they haul most of their people across the river by raft to reduce the number of trips. When it does cross, the new trolley car still rides the old cable, strung across the river and anchored to a boulder the size of a Volkswagen my father and grandfather buried deep in the earth.

Grandma Tommie was my step-grandmother, if that is a term people use. My dad's mother—Grandpa's first wife—lived alone in the Salt Lake Valley, about twenty minutes from our house. On Sunday afternoons, we would pile in the primer-gray van and negotiate the stoplights and intersections across town to her small home. A plate of cookies was always waiting on the table. Her home was modest, but her backyard was a wonder of flowers and garden. In high summer it looked like a private sanctuary. The space was limited—a small oval lawn flanked on all sides by dozens of different flowers and shrubs, the whole thing boxed by a chain-link fence. The smell was sweet and wet. The flowers were cultivated and proper. Grandma worked for hours—crouched or kneeling under a wide-brimmed sun hat—spreading top soil and peat moss, spading wild weeds, and trimming bushes, taming branches into place. There were always a handful of spray bottles just inside the backdoor. My brothers and sister and I would commandeer the bottles and turn the nozzles to force the water into a tight stream. Then we would chase each other through the flowers and the lawn, the old garage, the basement, and around to the front of the house firing beams of water and laughing.

As a child, I never thought much about my grandparents being split up. Yet some part of me seems to know that my grandfather entered into an agreement he could not live up to. He was a wild raspberry patch on the side of a mountain, and she was a flower garden in a concrete city. I've no doubt that she tried her best and that his stubbornness carried him away in the end, away to a place where he felt more at home, perhaps more alive—but certainly more apart. A place where a man could forget about his mistakes while killing rattlesnakes with a shovel—or fishing for steelhead.

One interior wall of the Stump Ranch cabin was devoted to cowboy hats and fishing rods. When we arrived, we were allowed to select a hat from the wall and wear it for the rest of the week. The rods were spinning and casting rods. The fish in the river had to endure ice jams in the winter, raging muddy flows in the spring, and bathtub-warm water in the peak of summer. Most of the hatchery trout died quickly or were harvested. The river was left to the northern pikeminnows and the steelhead.

Grandpa bought the cabin for the fishing. One corner of the front room was dedicated to photos of steelhead—often pictured in groups of four or five. Black-and-white images of my grandfather and my father (with hair?) grinning from opposite ends of a stringer, the fish spread out between them, cleaned and gutless, throats cut, massive jaws turned up at a forty-five-degree angle. As a teen, my newly minted catch-and-release sensibilities didn't know what to make of all that death, and my self-indulgent rock-and-roll angst didn't know what to make of those men. But I looked longingly at those fish.

More than anything, fishing was the line that ran through the men in our family. My grandfather taught my father to fish steelhead. My father taught his sons to fish for trout, because no steelhead ventured close enough to our city home to make such fishing more than a dream or a once-a-year excursion. As we grew older, fishing tied my brothers and me together. We taught ourselves to tie new flies and how to double-haul a fly rod. We loaded up our own cars in the dark blue dawn and drove our father to rivers flung across the West. All of this was in front of us when we pulled ourselves across the trolley each August. Without the Stump Ranch, those trips would probably never have taken place. The Stump Ranch was the place that showed us the hows and whys of wildness. Those pictures on the wall signified possibility while simultaneously telling us where we came from. We were anglers; that was clear. We were left to decide how to fit ourselves into that tradition. Those pictures let us imagine what had happened before and what might come next.

The year they built the cabin, my father would walk down to the river in the evenings with a casting rod. The rig of choice was a lead weight the size of a healthy night crawler, trailed by a spin-n-glo and an actual night crawler or a classic steelhead fly like a green butt skunk. He would stand on the gravel bar beneath the trolley and fling his line out into the swift current, let the heavy lead drag the rig toward the bottom, and hope. That fall he hooked a fish nearly every night. Grandma Tommie would come down and cast the same rig and catch nothing. If you include my grandfather, the three of them must have fished that gravel bar a thousand times. But it didn't matter because steelhead are so different from trout. For a steelhead, that section of river was merely a waypoint, a rest stop on a thousand-mile journey home. If those fish won't eat the green butt skunk today, don't worry; there will be new fish in their place tomorrow.

When I was twelve, my grandfather and I stood on the sun-bleached river stones and dried moss of that same gravel bar. Given the time that had elapsed and the nature of freestone rivers, the bar's location was nominally the same, but the stones under my feet were certainly different than the rocks my father stood on those fall evenings when he came down after a day's work on the cabin. Over the years, Dad's rocks had been picked up by runoff-tinted water, muddy and cold, and carried to some pile downstream. New rocks tumbled from upstream, and the river lodged them into my grandfather's gravel bar, beneath the trolley platform, across the river from the primer-gray van.

That morning on the riverbank I was casting a spin-n-glo and a worm to indiscriminate patches of river. It was high summer, and the rocks were nearly white from the sun, from the high spring flows that scoured the riverbank then left it naked as the water receded. Crickets buzzed in the sage and the day was working its way toward a dry desolate heat. Behind us the trail snaked up the hill to the cabin.

We were there because I wanted to go fishing before we left the cabin for another year. The pictures on that wall must have done something to me that year. I wanted to go fishing and he was my grandfather, so he took a rod down from the rack and pulled a can of worms out of the fridge. We walked down the hill, past the rusting jeep, around the old outhouse, to the bank of his river.

I remember Grandpa smiling at me and at the river from under his sunglasses. Thinking of that moment now, I imagine him recalling some evening with my father, maybe noticing how my brown hair was the same shade as my dad's, how mine cowlicked over my right eyebrow just like my father's—back before he went gray and bald. I imagine he was thinking about nights on that gravel bar, of fish lost and landed. I imagine he was even fleetingly carried back to moments and places that framed my understanding of him: the old house in Midvale with the flowers and my grandmother, the front seat of a Studebaker pickup, the night stars gleaming over Middle Fork Peak.

Thinking of that moment now, I want to think it was somehow significant for him, but of course, I am only guessing. Perhaps he was smiling simply because it was a beautiful day in a place where he felt at home. Maybe he was glad to be away from the noisy cabin that was usually so quiet when it was just him and Grandma Tommie. Maybe he was happy to hear the sound of the river, the background music for so much of his life. I don't know. I do know that moment has stayed with me. That morning always resurfaces when I think of him or hear his name at family reunions. I know that moment in that place somehow connects me to him now that he is gone, stretching like a trolley cable or a fishing line across history and memory from myself to my father and on to the lined, smiling image of my grandfather. To me, that day is one intersection in the spider web of my own identity, a complex map of who I have become: a father myself now, a fisherman, my hair as gray as my father's, yet still a boy casting into an unpredictable, opaque river.

The worm and the spin-n-glo were well out into the milky-green water when the fish took and leaped in a rush of spray, bucking like an angry horse. My heart sped and my mind lost its bearings and I convinced myself for a moment that it was someone else's fish. This was madness because Grandpa and I were alone and Grandpa wasn't even fishing. I felt the pull and I set the hook, but when the steelhead jumped, arching above the river's surface for a moment and forever, it didn't seem possible that it was my fish. It didn't seem connected to me at all.

But we were linked. For a mere second that is in memory somehow both an eye's blink and an eternity, I was tied to that fish. I was expecting a ten-inch trout or a pikeminnow. But this was a steelhead, an ocean-run rainbow trout maybe two or three times more powerful than any fish I had ever hooked or landed. A fish that traveled a thousand miles coming and going, leaving and returning home. A fish as wild as the wilderness that rose up the mountain behind us. As wild as the bear muddying the spring, as the rattlesnakes in the raspberry patch. A fish that had somehow negotiated four dams on the lower Snake, had paused a beat at the mouth of Salmon River before sensing the familiar and bursting into its home stream in a magnetic rush to a square yard of riverbed somewhere upstream where it was born and where it would die. A fish not unlike the rows of fish in the photographs on the cabin wall, framed by grinning younger versions of these two men whom I loved and revered and wondered if I really knew. A fish not unlike my grandfather, who needed wild places and cold water and chafed under the collar of civilization. A fish unlike any fish I had hooked before or since.

And then—in another blink—it was gone, back to the river, back to the wild soupy green of the Salmon's deep current, back to the ocean for all I knew. The rod went dead, the line limp. I reeled up, too confused to be angry.

"That," my grandfather croaked with a grin from beneath his hat, "was a real fish."

THE DARK

It's like walking down the hall barefoot at midnight through a minefield of children's toys, with the lights off.

That's the best metaphor, I think. That tiptoeing in darkness, down the hallway or across the front room. Each step is fraught with the possibility of pressing the flesh of your foot into something painful—a Lego with an infinite numbers of sharp angles, a high-heeled shoe raided from your wife's closet, a princess tiara.

There is fear in that walk, the sense that something is coming. But . . . when? That is what fishing in the dark is like. Casting. Stripping in line. The night sounds amplified, the moon on the water. More stars than you can fathom. And if you're lucky, that sudden violent yank of a good fish trying to kill and eat your fly simultaneously. There is something about the lack of sight, the relative blindness that both heightens your other senses and puts your brain on high alert. It is coming, but you can't see it (you can't see much of anything). You can only wait for the take: a moment of brutality that shatters the stillness. You can feel the power of the river snaking its way up the fly line into your hands. You can almost feel the trout hunting, ready to attack. It is coming, but . . . when?

My first time night fishing came on a small farm reservoir north of Logan. My good friend Jon and I were trolling in float tubes about twenty feet off the bank, a few weeks after ice out. Trolling is a good choice at night because—important words of wisdom coming here—it's hard to see in the dark. So the less you have to do the better. If you can minimize casting (especially casting any real distance), or wading, or any other verbs, you can last longer. But the more you cast, or try to change flies, or walk around with slack line at your feet, the more likely you are to create a bird's nest or tangle your feet in the line or trip on a stump. If you do get tangled, you will probably make another two dozen blind casts with that mess in your leader before you realize that you're tangled. Then you'll probably call it a night.

So we were trolling, kicking along the bank in the darkness of spring, talking to break up the night. Jon was swearing to me that I would catch a fish soon. He had hooked one already. I was blowing hot breath onto my fingers to keep them warm. The rod was lying on the float tube apron.

Then the fish struck.

The rod moved as if alive, the reel sang a little. Thankfully, I grabbed the whole rig before the trout pulled it into the lake. The reel sang true, my heart nearly exploded in my chest, and Jon got a good laugh out of the whole thing. After I landed and released the big rainbow, I started to worry about frostbite. It was very cold.

Since then I have tried fishing in the dark repeatedly on rivers, with mixed success. Obviously you cannot troll when you are not moving, you can only cast and strip. Or if you are uber-talented—I am not—you can fish dry flies and try to set the hook when you *hear* the rise. It can be done, and some very good fishermen—and probably some mediocre ones—do it all the time. My younger brother seems to be some kind of savant at this kind of fishing. He often doesn't start fishing until the sun is hitting the horizon and heading lower. Not me though. It's hit and miss for me. Maybe I have bad hearing.

River fishing in the dark is complex. You have to cast into an area where a fish might see your fly, and you have to retrieve, then cast again, maybe move up or down the bank if the fishing is slow, vary your retrieve, and if you are brave maybe try a double haul. All while relatively blind. I usually end up with a tangle if I am fishing two flies in the dark, so I always cut back to one, and if I am lucky I can fish for an hour in the blackness.

And it can be unforgettable. There is that last hour of light—the magic hour that is written into fly-fishing legend. But that first hour of darkness can be just as good, and there's that whole fish slamming my fly in the dark and sending my heart racing off the monitor thing, which is nice.

There is something about a wild place in the dark. It reveals itself in a way that is half threatening and half vulnerable. Large fish are there for the catching; beavers venture out and crash the water without warning, trying to run me out of their territory. I can almost feel the animals that have come out to hunt and the animals that are seeking shelter. This is not the same place it was at high noon. The river corridor reveals itself in new ways that are shadowy and mysterious, as if the land has peeled off a layer of day and exposed itself to the black and gray world of moonlight.

Packer and I once hiked several miles in the dark in the Uintas. We had arrived at the trailhead after dark, and we embarked in the moonlight, our paths lit by headlamps. We stumbled our way to what we thought was our destination and set up camp—only to arise the next morning and find we had missed a trail junction and camped at the wrong lake.

I like to fish the South Fork at night in the fall when the water is low. I often start by wading or hiking downstream in the evening light somewhere between a half mile and a mile (we all have our favorite holes, and few of mine are near the road). So when I am ready to go home, I end up walking out in the dark. I remember bushwhacking out through some very thick stuff by headlamp once with my brother, hoping neither of us broke an ankle or a leg or spooked a moose with a calf. Another time, I made a white-knuckle river crossing in the dark with a good friend. We simply locked arms and went where we thought it was safe. We made it. Looking back that seems like luck or divine protection.

I read recently that often the best fishing occurs an hour or two after dark, when the dusk light has surrendered and all luminescence comes from the moon (if there is one) and the stars. I want to try this fishing but haven't yet. I want to cast a streamer into a brown trout river in the heart of darkness. I want to surrender my eyes and rely completely on touch and sound and maybe some innate connection that comes up through the river water lapping at my ankles. I need a partner for such fishing because—let's face it—I am a liability if I venture out into that black world alone. I am pretty sure Packer will go with me.

I think it's all worth it. All those complexities and oddities associated with night fishing seem to scare off most normal fishermen. So the night belongs to the real fanatics. There is something nice about being in that club, even though there probably shouldn't be.

Sometime late in 2010 it started to snow in the Idaho and Montana mountains. The snowpack piled up, and anglers looked forward to the spring fishing. When spring came, it rained in the valleys and snowed in the mountains. April was a rush of rain. The snowpack was referred to in news reports as "well above average."

The idea of average in regard to fly fishing and snow and weather and life in general is—to me—something of a red herring, at least in the way we tend to interpret the word. Our perception of an "average" water year convinces us that such a year is quite common, but the opposite is actually true. Various instances of nonaverage years combine to form a statistical average that as an individual occurrence is not that common at all. This, of course, is how statistics work and shouldn't surprise anyone. The problem, I find, is that this phenomenon makes the business of prediction a fool's game simply because our conscious minds attach a connotation to the word "average" that leads us to believe that this year will be an average year, when it most likely will not.

As trout anglers, we tend to plan our years around occurrences of wild phenomena—pre-runoff skwala hatches, ice-off on your local lake, salmonflies and hoppers, prespawn brown trout so angry and horny they can't help but smash any minnow that enters their field of vision. We need these things to happen so that the things that we want to happen (i.e., catching many large trout) will happen. But all of these happenings are dependent on variables that cannot be controlled—water temperatures, the speed and ferocity of snowmelt, the length of the grass along the riverbanks in a given year, the high temperatures in western Montana each day for the month of April, the rate at which the ice on the lake melts, the water clarity when the stoneflies come off, the weather on a Wednesday in July. Wildness is inherently complex and unpredictable—this is one of its most endearing traits.

Such complexity makes the aforementioned occurrences (all those events that make for good fishing) difficult things to set your watch by. Such knowledge should lead fly anglers to distrust all predictions, especially hatch charts and descriptions of how a river might fish any more than about three days from the verifiable present. Predictions are an invention of civilization. From the almanac to the mock draft, they are humanity's way of attempting to think ahead of nature. In some ways, they are an attempt to domesticate what is wild. Unfortunately, our lives lend themselves to relying on such things. Life often forces us to plan more than three days in advance. We do the best we can. We often fail.

All of these items—the concept of average, man's attempts to predict (and thereby domesticate) nature, unending complexity, and our individual needs and desires to comprehend and out-guess that complexity—combine to make planning a fishing trip more complex than we are willing to admit. Take, for example, the Mother's Day caddis hatch. We insist on calling it that, even though it rarely occurs Mother's Day weekend. People show up that weekend hoping (even expecting) the caddis will be out and fish will be rising. The guys behind the counter at the local fly shop respond dryly that the hatch has been over for a week or two or three or that it won't happen until next week or a month from now. The Mother's Day caddis do not (generally) hatch on Mother's Day. They did once or twice, enough times to co-opt the holiday's name, and likely they will again. But you and I probably won't be there when they do because things are never as simple as their names.

This is one of the hidden advantages of quitting your job and becoming a troutbum and one of the ways in which the deck is stacked against the blue-collar angler. Few working stiffs can drop everything and hit the river the minute the first salmonfly happens to get eaten on a river five hours or two states away. There are schedules and people depending on us, which brings to mind this bit of sage advice from a fishy friend of mine: "Don't let people depend on you. It never works out." So we are left planning, months or even a year in advance, trying to time some hatch that has so many moving parts it might as well be a perpetual motion machine. Inevitably, we miss.

I am not a troutbum, but I do live close to some serious trout rivers, and I can occasionally drop everything when the first trout rises to the first large bug. Generally, such days lead to good fishing. But in the summer of 2011—the summer that followed the heavy winter and the wet spring, leading to a snowpack that was "well above average"—I realized that average isn't at all what I was looking for. While much of that winter and spring snow was barreling down the lower Henry's Fork as gallons and gallons of tea-colored water in early July, something important and unique and altogether not average happened. Something that showed the river and its wild heart in a way I did not expect. Something that now sometimes wakes me up at night, my mind churning and wondering when it might happen again.

Green drakes—those big succulent mayflies of summer—hatch more or less every year on the Henry's Fork and have a mainstream audience. The green drake is the drake they write books about. Jack Dennis's fly-tying manuals tell tales of fishing the greens on the ranch with a size ten Adams colored olive using a 1970s Sharpie. Nick Lyons's *Spring Creek* describes the first sight of the green drakes as a moment an angler feels "electrically, even when there are no fish showing" (1992, 35). He tells of taking a trophy brown trout, a fish unlikely to eat a small mayfly, on a green drake dry fly in a narrow strip of water—a fish that had changed its behavior for the occurrence of a bug whose size fell outside the average.

The green drake is the big fly of the sophisticated dry-fly angler. It does not abide the frenzy of the salmonfly or the cult of *Hexagenia*. It hatches during the brunch hour. If mayflies wore jackets, the green drake would wear tweed and look down its nose at the nocturnal brown drake and the wandering gray.

Those brown drakes also hatch every year on the Henry's Fork. On the ranch, the bugs bring out a cord of anglers and fish as the sun sinks low. Brown drakes hatch at night, and to me they seem larger than their green cousins. They are delicate, helicopterish insects. Their spinners return to lay eggs at the same time the duns emerge, filling the air with thousands of brown-and-tan mayflies, many of which end up lighting on the surface like it's an aircraft carrier, then laying down their long thin wings in a fatal egg-laying ritual than ensures the hatch will be on again next year. While the green drake hatch might last three hours, the browns mate and hatch and spin in a great rush, starting as soon as the sun eclipses the horizon and shadow takes the river. As the world goes dark, the trout become more aggressive, less fearful of open water. Walking away from a river lit by stars and moon, it's common to hear large trout rising gleefully to spent brown drakes, taunting anglers who have been unable to see more than a few feet for at least an hour but have cast on into the darkness relying on hope, intuition, and the sound of rising fish, rooted to their spot by the magic of a big fly and big trout.

Gray drakes are the oddball uncle of the drake family. Their hatches are inconsistent at their best and extremely localized, almost nonexistent, and confusing at their worst. Unlike their cousins, gray drakes do not hatch in the river itself. Rather, the nymphs swim to the banks and hatch in the river grasses like a stonefly that crawls out onto a rock to shed its skin. This makes the hatch maddening and unpredictable—more like a lottery or a shooting star than a hatch. A river needs the right kind of bed for the nymphs, grass along the shores, and a high-water year to push the river into the shore grass, allowing the nymphs easy access to the stalks where they will emerge and dry their wings. If nature checks all these boxes, the gray drakes will hatch. But unless there is a renegade trout that likes hanging out in the grass, gray drakes don't get eaten on the surface during the emergence like most mayflies.

But they are vulnerable when the egg-laying spinners return to the river to deposit their offspring. And if brown drakes seem bigger than green drakes (which they do to my unscientific eye), then gray drake spinners seem larger still. Maybe it's the scarcity of the bug that makes it grow larger in the mind. If I go for a month without seeing a trout, suddenly a foot-long rainbow seems pretty substantial. Perhaps this is the way it works for drakes. The trustworthy green drakes are seen most often, with the night owl browns just behind, followed by the elusive, seemingly massive gray drakes.

Perhaps it's all a trick of the mind, this size difference. Or maybe gray drakes really are bigger bugs. Everything seemed bigger that year when the river swelled from the runoff and spilled out onto the river grasses, threatening to flood the fields and the highways and providing a hatching point for the drake family's oddball uncle.

The water really was the color of tea. Runoff had peaked and the flows were headed down, but the water was far from clear, even though most of the Henry's Fork is spring fed and there are two substantial dams that generally filter out any color. In the oh-so-elusive average year, the lower Henry's Fork clears in mid-June. But—as stated previously—average is for losers.

Perhaps because the water is generally so clear, the lower river rainbows don't seem to rise that often in tinted currents. Knowing this, I didn't have much hope when I scrambled down a river slope and saw the water's color. I noted the water edging into the grasses and something flashed in my mind about gray drakes. There were a few spinners fluttering in the afternoon sun.

"Too dirty," I said to myself, wondering if the fishing might be on upstream. Then I saw the trout.

The fish was four or five feet off the bank, rising from the bottom of a piece of water that, during regular flows, would be only eighteen inches deep. Now the water was at least double that, and the fish was climbing the water column, taking a nymph of some kind near the surface then settling back to the bottom, disappearing into the tea.

I blinked and swore—not out of anger, but awe and surprise.

Brown trout were then something of a rarity on the lower Henry's Fork. They would come out for the stonefly emergence every year, then they were a myth until the streamer fishing of the fall. This is no longer the case based on my own unscientific net sampling data, and I can't help but wonder if the rising temperatures—both water and air—aren't contributing to the rising number of brown trout and perhaps decreasing number of rainbows. Regardless, in 2011 I had caught only a few brown trout from the two-mile stretch of water I had driven to that afternoon. These brown trout had one primary characteristic in common: they were bigger than most of the rainbows I had caught.

This trout was larger still. This was the kind of fish that wouldn't be out in the open during the middle of an average afternoon, that shouldn't be eating anything but other fish, mice, and birds, maybe a kitten that spilled into the river. This was an alpha. This trout rose from nothing and went back to nothing, hidden by the water's color, not too different from its own.

I wondered momentarily if I hadn't just imagined the fish. Perhaps I was having a stroke or an aneurysm.

Then the fish reappeared and rose all the way to the surface where he ate a gray drake spinner with a contented spurt. I could see the curl of the hooked jaw.

I cursed again.

I was upstream of the fish and I wasn't sure I could make the cast without spooking the leviathan. So I scrambled back up the hill and walked downstream thirty yards, then scrambled back down. I worked up to a casting position and tied on a size ten parachute Adams. I stripped out line and made the cast, but it dragged right away. I worried I had spooked the trout, but I soon saw its large buttery side again. This was a fish on the feed in a way that surprised me. There was no economy of movement. No frugality of energy. This fish was fixated on feeding, even if it had to move three or four feet for a bite. A fish of this size shouldn't behave this way. A heavy fish requires more energy for every inch. Even these big drakes seemed small in comparison, as if this was merely a twelve-inch trout eating PMDs. This wasn't like any fish—or any fishing—that I knew well.

As I stepped out into the current to get a better casting angle, the river itself seemed foreign, as if I were seeing an old friend's lost brother, an approximation of something I thought I knew. The current was strong right off the bank, and steps I knew as easy wading now took substantial effort. I could make out my shoes on the reddish tan river rocks but not clearly. The big fish rose again, and I noticed another large trout rise upstream of the first, another fish that seemed to be a trout out of place and mind, a fish that should have saved its feeding forays for night's darkness.

I realized that I had stumbled onto a secret version of the river. I felt almost like an intruder. This was a visceral unique moment on a stream famous for its predictability. The Henry's Fork's spring water and dams make it as close to a model of consistency as one can find in a trout stream. This river is one where an angler can occasionally predict correctly, a river where anglers can live more than three days in advance. But not that year, not that day. I was standing in a river a thousand miles from average.

It was a river, a place that had opened itself up to me without vocation, without resistance. It was rare and wild and unsustainable. To find such places always or even regularly would suck some of the joy from this thing we call fly fishing, from this moment in which I was shin-deep. But to find them oh, so rarely—to peel back the curtain and snatch a glimpse of what hides behind, to see wildness lose its guarded nature and step out from the darkness—is something sacred and momentarily perfect, something we all should wish for at least once. Something to keep us alive and filled with hope.

I cast up into the first trout's path and watched as the fish made the now familiar climb to the surface and inhaled the fly. I struck and the line came up tight and I felt a trout larger still than I was expecting contort and shake its head with a force that frightened me. This fish felt like a dog trying to throw its leash. It rocketed upstream and leaped, showing a black-pocked golden side in the afternoon sun. Then it ran to the middle of the stream and arced around me, my reel screaming, water spraying from the line as it cut through the tea. The fish got downstream of me and held. I was sure that one more downstream run would end the fight and I would be the loser. I worked my way back to the bank and down to a point where I had a decent angle. But here the high water rushed the bank and careened back in under tree branches. I couldn't wade any farther downstream. The fish held and so did I. I tried to reel and the fish shook its head as if to say no. I backed off, then tried again, and the head shook again and stopped me. Then the trout moved downstream a yard, two, three, taking more line than it gave.

So I waited. And the trout didn't run. I applied pressure and the trout held out. I don't know how long it lasted. I can't remember how I even got the fish to budge and begin to give ground. I only remember its large kyped jaw breaking the water as I got the head up finally just a few feet from me and slid the fish into what seemed like a net too small.

The fish was the largest I have ever taken on a dry fly. It

looked older than the river. The jaw was kyped and hooked like a shepherd's crook. The eyes glassed, tired and worn. The fish's side and tail carved with the medals of a dozen battles with other trout or maybe ospreys or fishermen, maybe a younger version of me.

I held the fish in the water and waited for it to thrust away with all the force of its mammoth headshakes. Staring at its length and jaw, I wondered how many times I had fished that spot or another spot close when the fish had known of my presence, but I had been unaware. Had I cast to this fish when it was younger and more prone to rising? How many times had I spooked it as I stumbled upstream looking for riseforms? Had I once released a small fish that this fish had then ambushed and eaten? Had we somehow fished for the same trout?

The fish was old and tired and took a few minutes to recover before it edged off on its own, gills panting. I watched it drain back into the tea-colored water and disappear, and I found myself wondering if any of this was real.

I fished until dark and caught several more trout, one of which was nearly as big as the first. As dusk peaked, the gray drakes were thick as moths on a lantern, and the fish rose freely. I spent all afternoon and into the darkness unlearning the concept of average. I no longer wished that hatches were easier to predict or that caddis hatched on Mother's Day. All of this unpredictability means that possibilities themselves are the thing I most seek. I want to know the rivers of everyday so that I can understand how different someday—maybe someday soon or someday past—might be. I want those visceral moments when the land and water and weather, the ecology of wildness, line up to create an outlier that illuminates a wild place with an unfamiliar light. An event that awes or terrifies me reminds me that what the poet William Stafford wrote is true: "Those moon rockets have missed millions of secret places" (1998, 219).

Each year now, when the first snow comes, I think of that afternoon. I don't love snow, but I pray for it. I hate shoveling it, but it is easier now. I want the snow to pile up like miniature Tetons in the city parking lots. I want a wet spring and muddy water all through June. I want the Henry's Fork to spill out into the river grasses. I want another year like that one, or—even better—one just as unique and different. I know such years, such days, such places are out there. It could happen again. Never plan on it—just hope.

WIND, RAIN, AND SNOW

It helps or it hurts. Sometimes you wish for it, other times you decry it, curse it, hail its arrival, hail its absence, or hope that it sticks around but doesn't get any heavier. You hope that it doesn't turn to lightning or snow or sleet or hail. Most of the time, it does the exact opposite of what you wish it would do.

Weekend anglers like me are at the mercy of the weather gods. Fishing reports like to qualify things with statements like "as soon as this hot spell ends" or "once it warms up." These qualifiers are often followed by promises of all the fishing you've ever dreamed of. And if you are a guide or a troutbum or independently wealthy, you are happy in the knowledge that such fishing is only a change in the weather away. But for the rest of us, all those promises are just another way of saying you should have been here yesterday or tomorrow.

When it comes to fishing weather, rain is context sensitive. If you are waiting on the streamer bite, it's usually good to get some rain. If you are waiting on the hopper fishing to get started (or keep going), you want it to stay dry. If you are counting on a blue-winged olive hatch, you want the cloud cover and maybe a little drizzle, but a full on rainstorm can ruin the whole thing. And if you are backpacking and planning on living out of a tent for three days or a week, well, you better just plan on rain and wind and maybe snow or plague. Basically, the effect of rain on the fishing is as random as dropping a quarter in a slot machine.

What we miss, I think, is that such randomness is one of the reasons why we venture out to wild places in the first place. The weather in my cubicle is always the same: seventy-one degrees, dry, the air stale with a hint of what Thoreau called "quiet desperation" (1995, 7). If I want consistency in the weather, I stay indoors. When I venture out, I try to see the rain not as a burden to be borne but as part the experience of being outdoors, a signifier of earth's wildness. Rain is a link to wildness you can feel by simply walking out your front door and letting it fall on you, pelt you with its coldness. Stand in a hailstorm and close your eyes and you will find yourself physically and emotionally connected with nature in a very real way.

So rain should be celebrated. Trout streams are beautiful places by their very nature, but they are scarcely more beautiful than when the rain has just stopped and the trees and flowers are glistening and green, shining in the sun—maybe a trout or two is celebrating the end of the storm by feeding on the surface.

I remember one April day on the Henry's Fork with my dad and brother when we waited out a heavy rainstorm in the car, watching the river's surface get pelted with gobs of water. Finally, the storm died down to a misty drizzle and the blue wings arrived—much to the delight of the trout and the three of us. We fished in the drizzle all afternoon and walked back to the car through the wet grass and willows, smiling and praising the weather gods.

Even though rain is wildly beautiful, I generally find myself thinking about it in terms of fishing. We anglers hope for rain or sun to stimulate the fishing. This is reasonable. Angling is our primary goal. Our most vivid connection to wildness comes via the trout. When the weather hurts the fishing we curse our luck, curse all the troutbums and independently wealthy anglers who will be standing in the river when the weather does cooperate. But this misses the point. Wildness doesn't cease to exist because we aren't catching fish. We should stop cursing and look for a way to connect with the land and the water, even the sky. Sometimes that connection comes *from* the sky in the form of wind and rain. And—sometimes—it hurts like hell.

In 2006 Packer and I got the idea of hiking into the B section of Utah's Green River. We had looked at a lot of books and websites and fishing reports about the Green, and we knew that there were Forest Service campsites downriver for the boaters. We were not floating the river, but we knew there were several sites close enough that we could walk to them across Forest Service land. The catch was that we had to have some sort of device for our human waste, some sort of portable toilet. That kind of thing is usually heavy, and heavy is a curse word for backpacking anglers unless you are referring to fly reels. But we scoured the internet and found a cardboard toilet that satisfied the letter of the law and prayed we would be able to camp close enough to the one outhouse on the lower river that we would never need that cardboard human waste receptacle. In the end, all those toilet-related gambles worked out, which probably should have been our first clue that everything else was headed for trouble.

We arrived late Wednesday night and set up a bare-bones camp in a roadside campground, slept for three hours or so, then broke down our makeshift camp in a matter of moments once the sky began to lighten. Early morning found us at the trailhead signing in on a whiteboard for the first-come, first-choice campsite near the outhouse. The Forest Service worker laughed at our cardboard toilet and sent us on down the trail. An hour or so later we arrived, set up our tent, and went fishing.

Packer had fished the previous fall on the Green with a guide and had cleaned up. It was a perk of his job as an engineer. He spent a sunny day in a drift boat with the guide and a vendor from a heating and air-conditioning parts company. He mostly ignored the vendor and focused on how he could take every word the guide said and apply it to future fishing on the Green. We were fishing almost exactly a year later, and we were confident we were going to catch some fish.

For one afternoon, our confidence was well placed. Under the bright September sun, we managed plenty of trout casting big cricket patterns and attractors into the seams and riffles. For one of the few times in my life, the fishing on the Green was relatively easy.

Then the clouds gathered, and we figured we ought to eat some dinner. By the time we finished eating, it was raining and the wind was blowing hard enough to make me worry about the tent. It kept raining and blowing for the next two and a half days. When it did stop, and the sun finally arrived, the temperature dropped and the wind began howling and our back teeth ached from the cold.

During that sixty-hour rainstorm we more or less kept fishing. We tried big dries and caught nothing. We tried nymphs and caught nothing. We tried streamers (which took a few fish) and blue-winged olives (no fish) and even little tiny ants (I caught three fish on those little ants one evening, which we deemed a huge success). But the fishing was anything but easy. We even tried sitting it out in the tent, just so we could feel something other than wind and rain. But the (admittedly cheap) tent leaked, and we spent most of our time trying to keep our sleeping bags dry. Finally, that last day under the cold sun and amid the heavy winds, we managed to nymph up some fish on San Juan worms.

Maybe we had been punished for our confidence. Maybe it was the fishing gods or the weather gods or a phone call to God from our enemies. I don't know. But the rain was miserable, and the fishing was almost as bad.

Still, when I think of it now, I feel connected to that place in a way that days of golden sunshine may not have provided. We saw the land at its most unforgiving; we saw behind the Forest Service website version of wilderness into the brutal heart of its reality. We learned the surface of the river as riffled by wind. We discovered the weaknesses in our casts as manifest by coils of line limped out just beyond our shoelaces, collapsed by a thirty-knot gust as we made a forward cast. Any misconceptions about the romanticism of nature were laid bare before us. The wilderness was not a theme park set up for our fishing experience. It was not a calm sanctuary of contemplation. It was cold and exacting.

Too often fly fishing is portrayed as either the genteel sport of gentlemen or the next extreme playground of young twenty-somethings wearing flat-brimmed ball caps. But wildness cares not for our public relations version of the sport. Wildness cannot be swayed by rhetoric or high-quality photography. If we want to feel the hope of wild places, we must accept them completely, even when they rear up in a climatized fit and ruin our weekend of fishing. If it only took three days of wind and rain and missed trout to buy me that knowledge, I would consider it a fair price. But it took longer than that. It took thirty winters.

I often stop fishing around Thanksgiving and don't get out again until mid-January. The holidays are reserved for family, and the weather doesn't encourage fishing. If I am honest, I haven't always cared for Rocky Mountain winters. Too many days of arriving at work in the dark and leaving in the dark, missing the daylight altogether in my tomb of an office. After a month and a half I usually have cabin fever and I need to see the river, feel the current pulling me. So I go fishing—usually someplace I have fished before—but I always encounter a new landscape.

The snow changes everything. A coat of snow contrasts the river and the land, making the world a black-and-white photo. The leaves of fall that kaleidoscoped the ground a month earlier are corpses under a white sheet, and the margins of the world are distinct. Fewer colors, more focus. The tracks of a deer along the riverbank are written in bold letters. The world gets slow and deep. The trout move to the eddies of their world and hunker down as the water flowing through their gills drops close to freezing. The air on the stream is colder still, and the water steams each morning as the sun warms it. This wildness is beautifully dangerous. Frostbite and hypothermia await the angler who slips and ends up in the river. Wind chills will turn fingertips gray. Ice clogs the guides on every third cast. It's no summer postcard. This is a different shade of wildness—harsh and beautiful and perilous.

Perhaps the best example can be found in freezing fog that wraps the trees and grasses up in an icy crystalline coat. The land sparkles even in the dreary gray of clouds, and the world looks alien and stunning. A couple of winters back I raced across the southern Idaho desert to a favorite tailwater—a river I have fished dozens of times—and found the place coated with freezing fog and nearly unrecognizable. The thin black fingers of trees were glazed in a semitransparent layer of ice. They bowed under the weight and leaned to the river's surface. The clouds in the sky turned the river's surface black while the snow blanketed the riverbank up to the first wet rocks, which signaled a border between moving water and frozen.

I kept looking up from my line to gaze at this frozen fog. This was my first trip of the year, and the cubicle maze had drained me. I needed the river. I worked my way to a spot where the river split and wound around an island, forming a back eddy where one spring several years earlier I found a big rainbow eating midges and mayflies off the surface with such slow lazy rises that I wondered if the fish had fallen asleep while eating. Inside the eddy the river goes a deep green when the sun is up, but this day it was a heavy charcoal. The current pirouetted in tiny circles. Winter water, I thought to myself as I pulled the line off the reel and dumped a cast into the riffle above the deepest run. The indicator hesitated while I tried to mend the line onto the right slot of river. Then the whole rig caught the wrong current and raced onto the fast water a foot or so outside my targeted drift.

Two casts later I finally mended with just the right touch and the line, indicator, and flies meandered down the four-inch seam, tightroping between the eddy and the fast water like a pointe-dancing ballerina. Should be a fish there, I thought. A microsecond later, the indicator agreed. I raised my arm and felt the electric throb pulse up through the line, down the rod, and straight into my cabin-fevered soul. I realized I was connected to the land and water, even the hazy frozen sky, the ice coating the tree branches, in a way that I needed yet didn't know existed. I never would have made this connection had I waited for the bluebird days of summer or even for a sunny warm winter day. If I had looked only for the romance of nature and ignored its slow-beating winter heart, I would have stayed home and become more civilized, more suburban, less aware of the land and its many masks. I released the trout and said a prayer of thanks for the Idaho winter, and for freezing fog.

FUNERAL

I have twice pulled into the parking lot of a funeral with a pontoon boat and a trunk full of fishing gear. In my defense, only once did I have the boat mounted to the top of my vehicle where everyone could see it.

Both funerals were in honor of grandmothers. The first was my wife's grandmother. With the boat on top, I drew some strange looks from the in-laws. But the service was held just a few miles from an irrigation reservoir that held some rather large rainbow trout. And since my in-laws were well acquainted with me and my affliction, they probably should have expected as much. My wife handled the whole incident with grace.

The second funeral was my Grandma Tommie, who died in 2007. She and my grandfather hosted my family each year at the Stump Ranch, their cabin along Idaho's Salmon River. Thinking back I picture her on the cabin porch smiling, her hand shading the sun as we make our way up the hill. I cannot separate her from the pine-covered mountains that rose up behind the cabin or that milky-green river out front where I once hooked a holdover steelhead as a boy. She was angry in her old age and probably wouldn't have approved of the deflated pontoon boat stored in the back of my Pathfinder. But my grandfather—an angler to his bones—would have understood.

The funeral was in Salt Lake, and I left the cemetery for Idaho and home, stopping on the way to fish a small lake I knew well in college. It was late March—cloudy and drizzly— the lake had just iced off. Piles of wet snow huddled in the tree shadows showing a bright white against the desolate brown that dominates the Rocky Mountain early spring. Other than the snow, the landscape looked so drab one might think that forest green and sky blue had been removed from the color palette entirely.

I pulled the boat's frame and limp pontoons out of the truck and took to turning the pile of gear into something that would float. The sky was gray and there was a hint of mist. I inflated the pontoons with a double-action hand pump that made a wheezing sound with every stroke.

Within the hour I was ten feet off shore kicking the boat along a stand of willows, thinking alternately about my grandparents, life and death, still-water fishing, my parents, my wife, my kids, previous trips to this lake, old college fishing buddies, and whether it might rain (and what that rain might mean for the fishing). In short, my mind was churning.

Then came the strike.

It was a single heavy pulse, a throb. Unmistakable in origin, it was gone almost as soon as it came. It lasted a millisecond. But in that instant all other thoughts vanished. My mind cleared and steadied, and I felt completely present for the first time all day.

I hugged the shoreline of a small bay. The trout were in close to the banks and the water was off-color, not unlike the Salmon River in spring. The fish came to a leech pattern, and I forgot everything except the happy, perfect business of catching trout for a couple of hours before I headed home.

I'd like to believe there was nothing symbolic in the trip—although I suppose that such an interpretation is a way of assigning meaning in itself. Still, I managed not to imbue those hours with thoughts of life and death and the significance of either subject. I don't know if that is necessarily a good thing. In the morning, I laid my grandmother to rest. That afternoon, I caught some trout. I suppose that sequence of events says something about my life, but for one afternoon I was perfectly fine not knowing what it was.

FEAR

On day two of a college road trip I stood over Ernest Hemingway's gravestone in the morning and nearly drowned that afternoon. Looking back, those two moments seem less important than what happened after.

Ernest Hemingway died in Idaho, in the upstairs room of a Sun Valley hotel. He put a gun to his head, and as he had done many times hunting birds and big game, he pulled the trigger. It was an act of violence to end a life that was constantly associated—and perhaps preoccupied—with violence. Hemingway died in Idaho, but I don't know how much he lived there. He certainly loved the Wood River Valley, but he spent his final years in the Gem State dealing with pain that he eventually decided was too much. He was a fisherman who loved trout and wild places. That much is clear from his work. He fished Silver Creek and probably the Big Wood River. He loved wildness, and I think he liked places and situations that felt slightly out of control—but that is pure speculation on my part. Maybe, as he got old, Papa Hemingway felt less connected to those things, I don't know. Maybe he was just drunk and hurting.

A roommate and I left Logan, Utah, in the middle of the night, drove three hours, and parked in an LDS church lot amid shadowy farm fields next to an abandoned car repair shop. We slept in the car until dawn woke us. We drove to Ketchum and stared bleary-eyed at Hemingway's marker—a massive granite stone surrounded by grass that needed mowing. Some wine bottles had been left on the stone as a kind of thoughtless tribute. The concrete spelled out little more than his famous name. As we stared at the stone I thought of ambulance drivers in World War I, bullfighters, and ancient sun-crisped Cuban fishermen. I thought of Europe and Michigan and the Florida Keys. And I thought of death and life and the strange dance between the two that Hemingway managed to describe using the perfect number of words.

Then we went fishing.

We stopped at a fly shop first. They pointed us to the Big Wood and warned us of high water but promised a few green drakes. We found a residential fisherman's access right there in town and began searching for big green mayflies in the current seams.

In "Big Two-Hearted River," Hemingway describes Nick Adams hooking a good brown trout on a sunken grasshopper: "Nick struck and the rod came alive and dangerous, bent double, the line tightening, coming out of water, tightening, all in a heavy, dangerous, steady pull. Nick felt the moment when the leader would break if the strain increased and let the line go" (1987, 176).

The words that catch me in this passage are "alive and dangerous." I've often thought about a linguistic representation of that moment, that sensation an angler receives in the instance a good fish takes. It is immediate electricity, the surge of life. Hemingway's description rings as true as any. The rod becomes "alive and dangerous."

I don't think it's a stretch to say that such moments—such connections—are a key reason why weekend anglers like me keep wading out into rivers and casting. It may be a cliché to say "the tug is the drug," but like many clichés it's grounded in some truth. That moment of life and danger jolts me from the aspects of life that lead to numbness. My day job—bound to a desk, no window, a maze of cubicles, arguments over lunch destinations—well, I won't say it makes me feel dead, but it doesn't breathe me full of life. Not the way the mountain air does or a glimpse of a creek through the trees or—especially—the moment a trout grabs my fly.

Fishing adds another sense to the mix, which is why it is so much better than simply looking. I think this is why people go rock climbing or kayaking: because they can feel the wild places on their skin, in their eyes. It is both visual and tactile. The simple act of that first cast to good holding water, feeling the line pulled back by the current, links me to the land and the river. That connection grows deeper and my pulse shifts into a higher gear when I see the smooth dark head of a good trout sucking down mayfly duns or the yellow side of a brown trout hunting my streamer.

In those moments, I stop thinking about being alive and simply live. All the world becomes secondary to the moment when the rod might become alive and dangerous. Wildness streams in and I strip line off the reel to make a cast.

We didn't find any drakes. We caught a fish or two on dries, then high water stopped us from barreling any farther upstream. So we backtracked a little and managed to cross the swollen river where a tree was down and stifling the current just enough to allow us to the other side. We fished up farther and caught little. All the while I was looking for a place in the river to cross back. We needed to get back to the car that was parked on the other side.

My companion was looking too. Finally, he decided we wouldn't find that second crossing. So he backtracked to the first spot and crossed again. Evening was coming, and I didn't want to lose the light and the time it would cost to double back, so I pushed on.

Bob Dylan could have been describing workday robots like me or a fly angler kept too long from the river or Papa Hemingway himself when he wrote that each moment is spent either in birth or death. This idea of fly fishing as a metaphor for life is central to the sport's literature. In his opening chapter of the masterpiece *Spring Creek*, Nick Lyons describes mornings spent watching the creek of the book's title. He waits until the fish turn from occasional risers to patterned feeders. Then he describes the seconds before walking down and casting: "As I looked from the suburban and then went out to meet it I always felt that the world and I were moments from being born" (1992, 13).

Lyons is touching on the same idea from Hemingway's description of Nick Adams's brown trout—the idea that fishing is a more lucid way of "being alive." What is left unsaid (except by Dylan) is the flipside of the coin: the binary opposite of feeling more alive is brushing death, or at least feeling that somewhere in the enterprise death exists. Sometimes life can feel like a slow death, the way a shallow creek dries up in a drought year.

We fish to keep that slow death at bay, to keep the water flowing. But in order to do so, we must glimpse death as well. There is a school of thought that we can only know something by experiencing its opposite. We learn to treasure happiness from experiencing sadness. We learn what light is the moment we flip the switch and all goes dark. Hence, to know life, we must at least brush up against death. In "Big Two-Hearted River," Hemingway's Nick Adams is back from war, from the land of death. For him, this fishing is a way to feel something other than death and loss, something alive.

Fishing—contrary to what we like to tell ourselves—is something of a blood sport, at least for the trout. In Hemingway's day, the angler almost always sliced the trout from anus to throat, fileted it, and ate it. Somewhere along the line we got smarter, started throwing a few fish back. This makes us feel superior in some ways, but catch-and-release fishing is certainly not bloodless. I've caught dozens of fish maimed by anglers—the trout lips gone from what I assume are guys just like me who had a hard time turning a fly out. These fish go back to the river perhaps wiser but certainly scarred.

Anglers in the 1940s and 1950s considered themselves top-of-the-food-chain predators who caught and ate fish for meat. Today, we turn trout back into the current and let them swim under the auspice of concepts like sport and conservation. I believe this is progress, and I am not arguing against catch-and-release ethics (which I think are important factors in the quality of today's fishing in the West), nor am I arguing that killing fish makes us somehow enjoy fishing more (which seems ridiculous). However, a fish that has been caught and released is not the same as a fish that has never been caught at all. And killing a fish is not always the sin some would make it out to be.

I watched the internet work into an uproar several years ago when a local fly shop owner killed a big brown trout on the Madison. This was the fish of a lifetime for an angler who had done more than his share to preserve the river he was fishing. Still, the catch-and-release zealots deemed him a "poor example." They virtually stoned him in a fit of self-righteousness, claiming we shouldn't support his shop and hurling unfair accusations behind a shield of anonymity. The whole thing had the feel of a holy war or a crucifixion.

But catch and release is not a religion, at least not for me. And while practicing it may reduce angling's violence, it doesn't make fly fishing a blood-free sport. Somewhere in the shadowy corners of our souls, we know that every fish we release might turn belly up due to the stress and situations inherent in fly fishing. And we know that sometimes killing brook trout that overpopulate a mountain lake is good for the ecosystem—especially since an airplane probably dropped those fish in the lake in the first place.

In those same shadowy corners, maybe we know that the rivers and lakes, and the wild country they run through, could kill us just as easily as we might kill those trout—by accident or by our own incompetence or arrogance or recklessness. I remember stepping down a boulder field in the Uinta Mountains with Packer. As I stepped off a stone the size of a Volkswagen, the boulder shifted a bit then settled. Had it moved more it could have pinned my leg. We were twelve miles from the car. I might have died there. Such moments change us in subtle ways, not unlike those trout we catch and release.

The river was full of sweepers—downed trees that would eat a boat if the Big Wood was big enough to float. A boat or a person that floats into a sweeper can be shoved subsurface then held under by the arms of a tree. Above one sweeper, the river riffled over gravel and boulders before it made a pool. I stared at the riffle long enough to convince myself I could make it across. I ignored the sweeper that bisected the pool below me.

So I set out. The water was only at my shins, but it was strong. Runoff still tinted the river, though it was late June now, and the current was stronger than I expected. Still, the point of the current was shoved near the far bank. I was more than halfway across now. I would make it. I was sure. I pushed on, and the water lapped over my knees and tugged my feet downstream. I tried to angle with the current, but the sand and gravel were starting to give way as the riffle's topography gave way to the pool below—the river was higher on my waders now and the sweeper loomed below me.

As I hit the point of the current, the sandy river bottom gave out and my feet washed from beneath me. I was turned over so fast that the tip of my rod went straight into the river, all the way to the bottom, and I felt the rod bend and snap.

Then I was in the river. On my knees, pushing off the bottom with my feet, closing my mouth against the rush of river water, fighting the current, trying to stand, scraping the bottom with my boots as the sand kept digging out from under my feet and refusing to let me stand. I tried to find a rock to drive from, struggled to keep my head above the surface and catch my feet as I was pulled downstream. I let go of the stumped rod handle and used both hands. I half swam and half crawled to the bank—coughing up river water as I pulled myself onto the gravel shore.

I sat down and tried to stop shaking, tried not to look at the sweeper—that aspen tree cut down by the current splayed across the river with its branches spread out underwater and above, where I might have been pinned had I not managed to make it across.

I was shaking. I felt alive, but I didn't particularly like the feeling. I had just survived my own stupidity. Hemingway's words "alive and dangerous" are as true for rivers as they are for a good fish hooked. I sat on the bank and knew it. I hated myself for making such a mistake, and for losing a rod to the river and my own false sense of superiority. I've replayed those moments in my mind a thousand times since: the feeling of helplessness as my feet were swept from beneath me, the crack of the rod as its tip was forced into the river bottom, my wet clothes clinging to my shaking body as I crawled up the bank.

The first inkling may have been back there outside of Cedar City when I realized that a drinking bull wasn't without danger. But in truth, I've always been something of fearful creature. In elementary school I was constantly afraid of getting beat up. Looking back, I wish I would simply have gotten beat up so that I might realize it wasn't that bad, that my fear was perhaps misplaced.

When I was thirteen on a Boy Scout trip, my tentmates and I were causing some sort of trouble that led us to roll the tent over on its side—flattening the door on the ground. Somewhere in my brain, the fear snapped into place. A feeling of being trapped in that dark, closed space panicked me. I shouted at my friends to roll us back over. I lost my cool—a sin for a thirteen-year-old boy on a scout trip. I looked weak and small, but I didn't care. I needed to feel the cool air of the world outside that tent. Eventually we rolled over (I am still not sure how we didn't snap a tent pole). I unzipped the door and breathed in deeply and tried to slow down my headless chicken of a heart.

I have wandered out of backcountry campsites on my way to a fishing spot only to be overcome by the sensation that a bear was waiting to ambush me. I have gazed over the edge of mountain-side roads and imagined my vehicle tumbling down the vertical side. I have never been downhill skiing—the thought of that ski lift makes me nauseous as I type this.

In short, I have let fear dictate my actions more than once. Heights, claustrophobia, wild (and sometimes not-so-wild) animals—these fears led me to avoid situations in which I would have had to face those fears. I was okay with that, and I often still am. I was willing to be something of a coward because I didn't feel like I was missing out on all that much. I don't need to be a downhill skier; I'm a fly fisherman.

But after nearly drowning in the Big Wood, I was faced with a real problem—one that I couldn't hide from. I became a timid wader. I wasn't fearless before, but I was brash. I felt comfortable wading water that was up to my navel, even if that water was a knot too fast. I had been whitewater rafting and sailing. None of it bothered me much or gave me much pause. But that day on the Wood retaught me the lessons of the bull Packer and I encountered on that road outside of Cedar City. I was suddenly aware that wildness—especially wild water—meant anything could happen, and anything could mean plenty of trouble.

The Big Wood shied me of water. This was a problem because I longed to be standing in rivers and casting, understanding water and fish and feeling alive. Now I was afraid to wade stretches of river I had no trouble in before. I was worried to float any river in any type of craft. I spent one day in a canoe on a lake then swore them off as too squirrely. I limited my pontoon trips to local lakes on calm days, and even then I found myself gazing into the depths and noticing that I could easily slip off the rower's seat, crack my head on the way down, and drown. I thought entirely too much about drowning—the moment when the lungs take in water instead of air. I knew it was painful agony. I began to see all sorts of places where rivers and lakes, bad luck, and incompetence could conspire to end me. These were places I loved—wild places I needed to keep me going, fill me with hope. Now I viewed them with fear, and I hated myself for it.

I have always known, of course, that there are many, many ways to die in places wild and tame. Car accidents and poor eating habits are more likely to kill us than a river is. Cancer takes even those who do everything right, and if cancer doesn't get you, something else will. In wild places drowning is only one option—lightning strikes, bears, bison, a wrong step in a boulder field that leaves you crushed to death—all of these could do the job. If you spend all your time thinking about the ways to die, you will probably choose to stay in bed, and that lack of activity and the stress from worrying so much—well, it'll kill you. If we consciously try to identify all the ways we could die at any given moment, we end up paralyzed, which is a kind of death all its own. So part of the way we cope—part of the way we live—is by choosing not to think of those things unless they are excessively scary or dangerous or new. We hide all the other death-causing things in our subconscious, and we live by not thinking about them because spending all of our time thinking about them is a terrible way to live.

But my swimming lesson in the Big Wood River had upset that process. I could no longer lock up all those thoughts. I could no longer choose not to think about them when I approached a trout stream. And this was affecting my life as a fisherman.

Hemingway said something else that I think about now as I write this all down. He said: "Every man's life ends the same way. It is only the details of how he lived and how he died that distinguishes one man from another" (Hotchner 1966, x). I knew that I didn't want to die pinned to a tree under the surface of the Big Wood River.

But I needed to decide how I wanted to live.

There are dozens upon dozens of reasons to love wild places. They are often incredibly beautiful in ways that seem both haphazard and intricately designed. They are clean and free from the stresses of civilization and suburbia. They are home to creatures like bull trout and badgers, grizzly bears and golden eagles. There are far fewer humans around.

A reason I hadn't much considered was that they force us to face our fears rather than just bury them in our subconscious. This isn't something I am particularly good at. But wild places force us to decide what the hope that comes from being among the trees and mountains is worth to us. If we are to truly connect with wildness, we must accept its brutality as well as its beauty. To do so meant that I needed to overcome the corresponding fear. So I began to force myself into water that felt a little too deep, a little too fast. I took my pontoon down some tame rivers. Mostly I was just trying to show myself reason. *See*, I said to my irrational, unreasonable fear, *you didn't die. You aren't always going to die.*

Eventually I have gotten to what I think is a happy medium. I still find myself choked with fear a bit when faced with a big river. But I also find myself wading through water I would have shied away from a few years ago. I have even manned the oars of a drift boat on some big rivers—though nothing with any real rapids. I haven't let my fear of wild places overcome my desire to experience them. I have come to terms with the fact that feeling alive means—in some ways—feeling scared of dying.

Of all the things we might learn from the wild public lands of the American West, I think this is one of the most important. Wild lands have the potential to remind us of our heritage, a heritage of wildness itself in which life and death are more finely poised, more intricately woven, than they might seem in an office cubicle. If we are willing to confront the unceasing presence of death in life itself, we will surely value life all the more. We will be unwilling to throw it away or waste it or take it from others with so little thought. This is the good a little fear might do, if we can resist the instinct to fight what we fear with violence and rage as well as the mirror instinct to simply run from it and hide. Certainly tyrants and propagandists have weaponized fear in some terrible causes. Instead, I want to learn from it, learn how to avoid it, and keep it from paralyzing me. Such learning is perhaps best accomplished on public lands, maybe with a fly rod in hand.

"Are they rising down there?"

"No. Not really. I think I saw one a while back but it may have been an illusion, just a swirl of the current. Are they rising up there?"

"No."

"Any risers?"

"No."

"Me neither."

"I'm seeing a few bugs, but the fish aren't up on them yet."

"Same."

"Risers?"

"There is one."

"Yeah?"

"I think I put it down though."

"Still . . ."

"Crap. Missed one."

"That looks like a good fish."

"Took the dry."

"Hey, a double."

"It's slowed down up here. Are they rising down there?"

"No, not really. I think it's over."

FIVE DAYS IN THE WILDERNESS

Bull trout require colder water temperature than most salmonids. They require the cleanest stream substrate for spawning and rearing. They need complex habitats, including streams with riffles and deep pools, undercut banks and lots of large logs.

There was a time when bull trout . . . were wildly abundant in the six western states of Oregon, Washington, California, Nevada, Idaho, and Montana. Bull trout were once found in about 60 percent of the Columbia River Basin, but today, they occur in less than half of their historic range.

U.S. FISH AND WILDLIFE SERVICE

It took nine hours to drive to the trailhead. Not because the trailhead was located in another state, simply because much of the route was dirt and gravel and the last fifteen miles consisted of a rutted one-lane track that went up, over, and down a mountain. We listened to Bob Dylan and openly marveled at the country. The three of us—my father, my brother, and I—had been here once before, but the central Idaho mountains are stunning enough that memory cannot entirely contain them. There is some portion that can only be captured in person and must be surrendered when one reaches a paved road.

By the time we parked at the dusty trailhead, early evening was beginning to show, so we hoisted the packs, reset the GPS, and began walking, following a small tributary down to the main river. This was a downriver hike, and we followed the stream as it grew from an infant to a toddler. As the stream widened enough to make it interesting, we began pointing at holding water and grunting to each other as we walked. This was bull trout and westslope cutthroat country, two species that had been swimming here longer than we could fathom. We wondered hopefully about the shadows beneath stream-bound logs.

Stupidly, caught up in trout dreams, we didn't stop to rest or drink much water, wanting to make camp before the oncoming dark. My father was in his midsixties, and he had trained harder and more faithfully than either Justin or me, but the long day folded into the car followed by a paced hike with little food or water sapped him. By mile three he was stopping every quarter mile and taking off his pack. Sweat ran down his drawn face. By mile five I went ahead and found a camp spot, then came back for his pack. He walked behind me without speaking, keeping his eyes on the trail. We set up a tent, and Dad crawled in, feeling his age and probably wondering why he was out there. My brother and I kept the fire company and didn't talk much. A river of stars washed the night sky into currents and eddies.

I like to think back through five hundred years, before dams and reservoirs, before there were mines on every hill. It was then that bull trout were the dominant predators in streams throughout what is now called the West. The Fish and Wildlife Service calls them apex predators, and I can imagine that fishing for them back at their peak might have been the apex of angling experience. Bull trout are not vegans or predisposed to dining on midges. They prefer meat that swims. Stories about rogue bull trout trying to eat a twelve-inch cutthroat that is in the process of being reeled in are so frequent that they are no longer a novelty. You can watch it happen on YouTube. Like brown trout, bulls love structure: undercut banks and deadfall. Like native cutthroat trout, they need cold clear water they can traverse to spawning grounds. Like brook trout, they are really a char, and their backs resemble what Cormac McCarthy called "vermiculate patterns that were maps of the world in its becoming" (2006, 287).

But the world's becoming was hundreds of millennia ago, and the world of today is less tolerant of this apex predator. Clear cold water that flows freely is no longer the rule in the West. Bull trout have dwindled. In the face of a changing climate, they are holding on, but I worry about them. I worry about what losing them would mean.

When I do encounter them, they show enough to let me know they are not gone yet. They will slam a white streamer that drifts and pumps close to a drowned log, emerging from the shadow like a lion on the hunt. What if they still swam freely in those rivers close to town? What would the West have to look like for that to be true? What lives have they led all these millennia? What have I missed that they have seen? What are we losing as they disappear?

The next morning found me and my father bushwhacking through a meadow of grass so tall we couldn't see over it. This was a wilderness area, and we were now six miles or so from the car. At one time there had actually been a road that wound down this stream to a homestead and a mine, back before the Wilderness Act attempted to erase the road, which still shows in the two tracks the trail occasionally adopts through the landscape's meadows.

We left the trail and pushed our way through the tan-and-green stalks using the sound of the river as a compass. We broke out on a riffled run fragmented by several large boulders. On my father's second cast, a heavy westslope ambushed his stimulator. His face cracked into a grin as he guided the fish into the bank. After removing the fly, he held the trip's first trout in the water until it broke from his light grip and melted back into its ancestral home. Yesterday's hike seemed to drift downstream.

Westslope cutthroats once shared this stream with massive runs of steelhead and salmon before the dams on the lower Snake cut the flow of sea-going fish down to a trickle. These cutthroats have been avoiding ospreys and attacking stoneflies for eons. Beneath the surface the trout seemed to liquefy, their backs so patterned to the contours of river rocks that they became water. I watched my father smile through his white beard as the red-splashed cutthroat disappeared back to the wild.

I worked my way upstream and caught a few small fish in the pockets and slicks. After switching to a big hopper, I went looking for deep water. I found a long run that ran against an undercut meadow bank where the water slowed and riffled. It was a fishy spot teeming with cutthroats.

The first few fish came to a streamer as I worked the run from the top down. Then I fished dries back up to the top and took more trout. The numbers were nice, but the real prize was these fish dressed in their summer best. Brilliant orange and red, fish so bright that when they slipped back to the depths and disappeared I couldn't help but blink and wonder. Fish so colorful they should have been visible from thirty yards away melted into river bottom at three or four feet.

An hour later, I sat on a small island and ate granola bars for lunch. My father had walked back to camp for a nap. An osprey circled and lit in its nest a hundred feet above the river at the top of a dead, tilting black pine tree. The bird screeched, warning me off her territory. I was a hundred miles from the nearest paved road and six miles from the truck, low-holing an osprey. It was a nice lunch.

Bull trout used to swim in dozens of rivers west of the Continental Divide. If a river drains to the Columbia, it is a safe bet that it once held bulls. We can trace their decline to human manipulation of the land: logging, agriculture, dams. Scientists consider the bull to be a canary in the West's coal mine, an indicator of good water gone bad. The fact that bulls are listed as "threatened" on the Endangered Species List, the fact that you can no longer find these fish in California, doesn't bode well for those of us who live in the mine.

Bull trout live on in central Idaho, one of the places in the West where the landscape likely resembles its condition from five hundred years ago. Central Idaho is home to the largest roadless area in the lower forty-eight. This swath of land, accessible only by boat or horse or foot, is bisected by the Middle Fork of the Salmon River, where all the water we fished those five days was headed. Sentinel to that river, standing up more than ten thousand feet on the north side of the stream, is Middle Fork Peak, a knob of rock and snow rising to the sky. Perched on top of that knob is the wildfire lookout that my father and grandfather built.

Wildfire lookouts themselves are endangered because planes have become better tools for finding fires. But years ago my father spent the summer on that peak with his own father, hauling wood and cement up the last ascent with a pulley system they jerry-rigged out of a Studebaker and some lumber. He talks often of that summer, of learning who is own father was, listening to the Dodgers on radio waves that rode the stars from California. It was a period that defined him, in part because it allowed him to learn about the man who fathered him and about the places that meant something to that man.

As we fished those five days, I couldn't help but think that I needed my own summer to answer that question about my dad, that somehow during our eighteen years of living together I had missed him altogether. I had been so focused on my needs and wants and problems that I failed to realize he was anything other than my father. I had failed to understand he was an actual human with a life that took place before I was born. And yet, as the previous day's hike had shown us, trips with Dad were as endangered as the bull trout and the wildfire lookouts. This wild country where he had once stood watch was almost too wild for him now. His body and his forest had betrayed him. And we, his sons, were left to find the places where we could know him.

That evening, my father and I hiked back to that long run that held so many afternoon fish. I checked the knot on his stimulator and gave him the top of the run, what seemed the best dry-fly water. He turned the fly over neatly and dropped it into riffled water that must have held a dozen cutthroats if it held one. But the fish didn't come. I watched my father cast over perfect holding water with no reward. That great afternoon run was an evening mystery. I peeled the line off my reel and slung a streamer at the far bank in the lower half of the run. Six casts later I had a fish, then another. My father caught a small fish. Then we switched ends and he caught a nice cutthroat. It wasn't all I had hoped for, but it was enough. We talked about getting back to camp, about getting a good rest for the next day as I threw mindless casts against the undercut bank—working water that seemed strangely devoid of life, as if all the cutthroats had left before we arrived.

When the big bull finally ambushed my streamer, the jerk of the rod startled me. I didn't really set—the fish was just there, throbbing. I looked to the middle of the run, where my line disappeared, and saw the flash of the trout's side as I felt the headshake. I knew then this was no fourteen-inch cutthroat. This fish tried to eat fourteen-inch cutthroats. I tried to say something to my father, but the words crumbled in my throat and came out like the sound you might make if you were kicked in the chest.

The big bull shook its head like a horse trying to lose a bridle and burrowed into the deepest water in the pool. A downstream run would have doomed me, forcing me to chase the fish through pocket water and logjams. But the fish stayed put, stubborn for the deep undercut bank, shaking its head in defiance. The big bull wouldn't be moved, wouldn't give up its stronghold. So we stood in concert, connected by the line and the arching rod, the fly buried in the fish's hooked jaw, the sky turning to fire in the dusk, the wild country growing wilder into night around us, the Middle Fork and our family peak fifty miles downstream, my father grinning like he won the lottery while standing on the gravel bar beside me.

Finally the fish lost its will and eased into the back of the pool where the water was shallow, and I was able to guide it up into a pocket of still water. The big bull was otherworldly in the evening light, its orange spots catching the sunset as it turned on its side and posed for a photo. I snapped a picture through water so clear that the photo looks as if the fish is beached on the rocks rather than resting in ten inches of liquid bound for the Pacific.

I removed the size two double bunny from the corner of the trout's jaw and guided the fish back to the current, babbling uselessly the whole time, talking loudly and saying nothing. I remember my father looking down at me from the bank as I crouched in the stream, smiling through his beard, his eyes twinkling under his bucket hat. There in the evening light I wished suddenly it had been his fish—a great bull for my father on this trip, which might be his last into the backcountry. I wish he had caught this fish for all those years past, for all the bulls now lost to time and roads. I thought of him teaching me to cast on the back lawn, teaching me to tie a woolly worm in the basement of my childhood home, which earlier that year had been plowed under like so much bull trout habitat. But I couldn't make it his fish. And he took pleasure in watching me blabber like an idiot, at seeing that big fish move slow and powerful back to the wild river. As I guided that ancient predator back into the current I could feel the fish's gills rise and fall. Holding that fish was like holding the entire backcountry or the whole history of the West. I could feel the power as it pushed away with a tail flick and a head shake. The episode couldn't have taken more than a few minutes, but in memory it lasts for hours and plays on a loop.

Two days later I fished up the creek in the twilight. I was hoping for a few last cutthroats, maybe a final bull before we hiked out the next morning. We had hiked well downstream the previous day and fished together as a trio—my father drifting a stimulator through every hole, then my brother smashing big streamers against the banks and logs. I went last, dredging a rubber-legged stone nymph and a Tungsten Prince beneath an indicator, picking up a whitefish for every cutthroat and not caring at all. In one hole we each took a good cutthroat. We laughed and marveled at the bounty of the river, the gratitude we felt to be in that place on that day, together.

After three hours of good fishing, we crossed the river and climbed up a gravel bar adorned with a very large, very purple pile of fresh bear scat. It was berry season, and a sign at the trailhead had warned that the bears were along the river. We headed back to camp. The bear went unseen.

The next day we hiked halfway to the car, stopping in a meadow to camp and take one final shot at the trout before we packed out the next morning. Before the evening fishing, we swam in the creek and talked about next year's trip (destination unknown). My brother and I rigged up to fish, but my father declined. He was going to sit on the bank of the creek and soak his feet, let the cold wild water that was pristine enough for a bull trout renew him before we hiked out in the morning. He would watch the birds and look hard into the river, try to guess what was a cutthroat and what was a rock. I knew then that I would never share this backcountry stream with my father again. He was nearing seventy, and his lion's heart could only carry him so far. If he were to come the six miles packing forty pounds of gear on his back, he needed the legs and shoulders of his youth.

He knew it too. He may not have liked it, but he was at peace. He knew that his trips now were for the Madison or the Henry's Fork. He had seen more country than I could dream of. He had built the lookout and fished the Salmon River when the steelhead were as thick as the downed timber along the trail. He was okay soaking his feet and eating granola. He was connecting with the land on new terms, but he was still connecting.

I wasn't okay. I could feel civilization, time, and biology combining to reel me in, and I did my best to hold out and make a long downstream run. I could feel this trip with my father ending, unsure if it was enough. After a week in the woods, I was anxious to see my wife and daughters, I needed a shower, and I wanted a hamburger and a Coke. But I still wanted one more evening without turn signals and streetlights. I fished with desperation, trying to tattoo this place on my soul so that I would never forget the river, the mountains, the angled crisped pine trees housing ospreys, the bear scat, or the fish.

I didn't know it then, but I think now of how public lands have connected my father and I, our whole family even. We rode dirt bikes as kids on land managed by the BLM. We hiked into the High Uintas Wilderness area together and the national forest lands along the Green River in northeastern Utah. Public lands form a kind of network in the West, patchworking themselves from Canada to Mexico. This network connects the various wests—the Southwest to the Northwest, the Front Range to the Pacific Coast. Public lands also connect individuals. Sure, I have memories of my father at our home, tilling the garden, teaching me to cast a fly rod on the back lawn. But I see him most clearly, in pristine memory, flanked by the signature pine trees or desert horizons of the West's public lands. Nearly all of our best conversations have taken place on streambanks or around campfires or in cars in route to public lands. Some of those conversations required no talking whatsoever.

I fished hard that night, drifting a Parachute Madam X down every seam, yanking streamers through the deep holes. I caught a nice bull trout from under a log and lost an even bigger one from under the same log. I fished fast and reckless, racing the evening light, knowing that darkness meant the fishing was over. I cast poorly and missed strikes, skipped water unless it looked perfectly fishy to my eye. Finally, I slowed down enough to take a good cutthroat on a dry fly with a dropper. This trout was brilliant red along his belly, fat and healthy. I left him in the shallows and snapped a photo. As I reached down to release the fish, he jerked violently and flopped up onto the bank, stabbing the dropper nymph into my palm past the flattened barb to the bend of the hook. The fish flopped and twisted in the dirt and finally snapped the line. Then he managed to flop back into the water and swim away, my fly tucked in the corner of his mouth. I think I saw him smiling.

I dug the fly out of my palm and blood poured out behind it. I shoved my hand into that river and watched the red stream of blood clot in the cold water and cartwheel downstream. The blood formed a ribbon beneath the surface, tumbling along between the rocks, heavier than that clear water but not quite sinking, finally breaking up and dissolving into molecules as the river roared on toward the Middle Fork, the wide Columbia, the Pacific Ocean.

I sat on the bank and decided that this strange moment meant something. That I was a blood brother to that river now, to those mountains and that wild country—or at least that I was kin to that place in some way. I had given something to the river. I had mingled my blood with its wild heart. This river where we had spent five days with wildness, glimpsed it, felt it brush up against us, tasted it in water so cold it ached our back teeth, smelled it in the clear night air, found it in rainwater puddled in a bear track.

I hiked back downstream and sat with my father. We ate granola and watched the night sky take the dusk. The western horizon went blue then black, and a river of stars flooded over, carrying us away.

PAIGE'S TROUT

My daughters started the same way I had started: on the back lawn casting to a bucket. Rather than a fly, both of my girls were casting tufts of yarn. I was failing as a teacher. It was early summer, and the brilliant green grass contrasted the lined loops of orange and pink reaching languidly for the empty one-gallon that once held moose tracks ice cream.

The situation seemed straightforward. The girls wanted to go fishing with me; I wanted them to go fishing with me. Before that could happen, they needed to learn how to cast. I thought of Norman Maclean's father, the idea that the fly cast was a way of tuning oneself to God's rhythms. The idea that the fly cast itself was a kind of grace. He taught his sons to cast with a metronome. Maclean writes that, had his father been in charge of the rules of angling, "nobody who did not know how to fish would be allowed to disgrace a fish by catching him" (2001, 3). Maclean's father—a reverend—likened the fly cast to an exercise in grace and beauty, and he taught his sons to cast in that image—the image of God.

My own father wasn't nearly as serious about the sport. In some ways, my brothers and I converted him to fly angling. Before we got pious about it, my dad would use whatever method he thought might best tempt a trout: flies, gear, worms, salmon eggs—it was fair game if it caught fish. This was before we got caught up in the spiritual side of fly fishing, before I ever read Maclean's thoughts on Christ's apostles: "We were left to assume, as my brother and I did, that all first-class fishermen on the Sea of Galilee were fly fishermen and that John, the favorite, was a dry-fly fisherman" (2001, 1).

Although I was devoted, there wasn't much grace or beauty on my back lawn that day with my daughters. We didn't have a metronome, and we were lacking all rhythm, especially the divine. The girls seemed to be taking the rod too far past noon on the back cast (Maclean again: "Until man is redeemed, he will always take a fly rod back too far" [2001, 3]), but I couldn't seem to explain exactly when they should bring the cast forward because the clock metaphor was too abstract. When they did try to stop earlier they came forward immediately, in a rush that left the line a looped mess at their feet. I talked philosophically about letting the line "load" before the forward cast. Both girls looked at me as if I were unfamiliar with standard spoken English.

I wasn't sure my girls and I had learned enough about fishing to avoid disgrace, but weeks later my oldest daughter and I drove into the mountains on the flank of the South Fork of the Snake River and met a group of fathers and daughters for an overnight backpacking trip. I shouldered a pack with two sleeping bags and a tent while Paige carried her clothes and some food in a pack not much different than the one she wore to school each day. We walked four miles of trail up a creek that was trouty and lined with overhanging brush. When we stopped to fill our water bottles, I learned that the stream was teeth-achingly cold. I immediately wished I had packed waders for the both of us.

As I looked around, I began to feel both ancient and young. It was a place not unlike the Uinta Mountains of my youth. We were miles from the car. We had hiked with packs on our backs through wild country. We would camp near a lake where trout rose, drawing circles onto the glass surface. This was the abridged version of my teenage summers, and reliving it brought back the immortal feelings of youth. But there was one thing especially different: I was not trailing Packer or Justin; I was with my daughter. I didn't feel old enough or smart enough to have a daughter, so leading her into the woods felt like a dangerous situation. As I thought about this delicate human walking in front me, chatting with her cousin about horses, I knew that in her story, I was playing a role for which I felt ill-suited. I wasn't one of the brothers, Paul or Norman Maclean; I was Reverend Maclean. This new casting was something that I had forced myself not to think about until now, here on the trail surrounded by wild places full of grace, danger, and beauty. The roles had shifted. How long would it be until I, like the reverend, could no longer crawl down the steep banks to the best holes? Such things felt far off, but so had the role of fatherhood once upon a time.

My own father taught me to cast on the back lawn. He taught me how to bait a hook and tie a woolly worm. One of the clearest memories of my childhood is the day he carried me across a river on his back. Was I ready now to be the one wading rather than the one riding? The backpack filled for two that I was carrying seemed to be telling my aching shoulders that I was not. Still, we made it up the last hill and set up a ramshackle camp, five sets of fathers with tents and bodies in varying states of disrepair. Our daughters chased squirrels and skipped rocks on the lake. I found myself constantly worried I would lose Paige to the wilderness. I wondered about bears and moose. I feared the boulder field down trail from our camp. I worried about the teenagers that came through and set up camp nearby. At some point I stopped feeling young and just felt helpless.

As the sun scoped the horizon, I rigged up a rod, and Paige and I walked back down the trail looking for a pool or two that might give up a native cutthroat. We tried cold wading, but the pain of the water was too much for my daughter. She didn't expect fishing to be painful. I thought this was apt preparation for life, but I didn't say so. She crawled back to the bank and ordered me to catch a fish.

Upstream the water rushed to the far bank and careened off a boulder the size of a moped before plunging into a pool that glinted aqua green through the foam. The willows and cottonwoods loomed along the banks, waiting to latch onto any cast except one that was straight and narrow. I tied on a fly made of foam and two white calf-tail wings so that Paige could see it in the water. I wondered when my own feet would stop hurting from the cold, and then I cast. The fly landed on the foam seam and sat teetering for a moment before the current caught the line and dragged it away. Just as the fly began to rush downstream a fish slashed at it and missed.

"Oh, we had one go after it." I decided this was a team endeavor.

"Really?" she said. "I didn't see it."

"I'll see if I can get the fly to drift in the good spot a little longer."

"Try casting it farther up, closer to the big rock."

I wasn't sure how she knew, but she was right—that was the spot. So I threw it a little farther upstream by the big rock—onto a piece of water the size of small bucket—and made an immediate upstream mend. I pulled it off better than I expected. Reverend Maclean might have even approved when a trout's head popped up from the foam and inhaled our gaudy fly with abandon.

The fish ran all over the shallow stream in panic but never came unhooked. I reeled in and encouraged Paige to net the fish but she declined.

"It's too cold," she said.

So I netted the twelve-inch native and walked to the bank, where we let the net rest in the shallows and watched the fish. Paige touched the spots on the sides, and we turned the trout over and looked at the two brilliant orange slashes beneath the jaw that give the trout its name. We talked about the fact that this fish had ancestry in this river from back before there was ever a trail or a campground or a city or a house or a railroad in this part of the state. About how native trout are a thing to be treasured because they encapsulate something wild that we could never get back if we were to lose it. I told her that touching this fish as it rested in this river was like touching the whole West before Lewis and Clark showed up. She thought that was okay, but she was ten, so she said:

"I thought it would be slimier."

We let the fish go and it rushed back up to the only deep water in that stretch, the very place I had just cast to. Paige and I got back on the trail and went scouting for a spot where Paige could catch a fish.

We came to a stretch where the river had diverged from the trail. The water was walled off from us by a stand of willows and brush. Based on what we could see of the river before it turned, I thought we could catch a fish here. Paige was dubious, mostly because there was a stand of vegetation between us and the creek that looked impassable.

"How do we get through?"

"We can bushwhack. I'll go first and hold the branches for you."

She seemed unsure, but she followed me.

Maclean writes about "the hope that a fish will rise" (2001, 104). "Hope," of course, is a word pregnant with religious meaning; it's similar to "faith" but different. A fly riding a current seam is an embodiment of hope, "the thing with feathers" in Emily Dickinson's words, just like Wallace Stegner thought the public lands were an embodiment of our hope as a nation.

When one first begins to sort out fly fishing—the exceptionally long rod, the infinitely tangled lines, the algebra of leaders and tippets, the religious balance of the cast, the guesswork of fly selection, the mysticism of reading water—hope is a rock to lean on. How can all of these things, so awkward and inaccessible on their own terms, ever combine to catch something as beautiful and elusive, as wild and invisible as a trout? The best one can do in these situations is to go fishing, to keep casting, to keep hoping.

Wild streams are great storehouses of hope. They contain wild and native trout. They reflect light from water. They witness that not everything is measurable in a spreadsheet. These are reasons to hope and things to hope for. I remember backcountry evenings when a soft envelope of light would ease over the Uinta

Mountains. The circles of feeding trout seemed drawn to that light, trying to drink it in as they rose from the bouldered green bottom of a mountain lake ten thousand feet above the ocean. So many fish climbing to the surface and sipping the dusk, nipping the specks of bugs from the ceiling of their world, circles expanding and colliding until the lake itself looked pelted by rain, Packer and I checking the sky for clouds in spite of ourselves. We spent all day hoping for such moments.

As Paige and I forced our way through the willow branches, I knew that this was a moment where hope was needed. How long could a ten-year-old with a bad teacher for a father hang on to something as esoteric as fly fishing? If she didn't catch a fish or at least see a fish, frustration might set in. A thousand more interesting and accessible hobbies might steal her away from the thing that made me feel most connected, the thing I wanted to share with her and her sister. We were crashing through the brush, and I hoped we would find something on the other side, but I wasn't sure. There was no good reason that this stretch of water—assuming we could reach it—would give us anything. Paige could not wade this cold stream, something that I had not counted on. So were left with the hope that she could cast from the bank, that the willows and cottonwoods leaning in to hear the creek's roar wouldn't simply snare her offerings before the fly found the surface.

I held back branches and Paige ducked low, stepping into the brush.

"Are you sure about this?" She was losing faith in me.

"Nope."

"Ow. That branch cut me. Dad, I'm bleeding now. See?! Where is the water? Should we go back?"

"I think you'll live. It's just a scratch. I hear the creek now."

We broke out of the willows and into sunlight. This spot was brighter than the shadowed trail. The river sparkled and shone. The creek here cornered on a forty-five-degree angle framed against a massive rock opposite us, then boiled and braided downstream. But here, inside the corner's elbow, there was a graveled patch of shore free from trees and branches, a veritable platform for ten-year-olds who are unsure about their cast. And the river itself looked fishy. Foam lines and current seams bespoke of spotted residents beneath.

"Oh, Paige." I smiled and stared at the river.

"Does this look good?" That bushwhack through the trees had shied her.

"Yes. We want to cast just below that giant rock."

We settled onto the casting platform, and I readied the rod and line. I tried to force myself not to talk too much and to talk slowly when I did. I was giddy, though. I realized as I handed her the rod that I had never felt quite this way on a river, I had never had so much emotional investment in another person's chance to fish, never had so much hope wrapped up in something over which I no longer had any control.

"Remember—back cast, stop, then forward cast and stop. You want your fly to land at the bottom of the run here. We will fish up through the run."

"So down here by that rock sticking out?"

"Just downstream of that, yes."

She cast. Poorly. The loop of line above us collapsed. The thing with feathers landed in an inch of water at our feet.

"Oh, that was bad," she said.

"That's alright. No harm done."

I picked up the fly and blew the water off, then tossed it into the current where it floated down below her, straightening the line and giving her a head start on the cast.

"Try it again."

Paige picked the fly up with her back cast and made a serviceable start and stop that looped the line and fly out into the current in the general area we had discussed. Almost instantly a fish rose and hit the fly. Paige made no move at all.

"Oh, fish! Set!" I was shouting, my excitement unleashed. But the fly was floating again, the fish gone.

"What do I do?" She looked up at me.

Somewhere Reverend Maclean was probably documenting my disgraces, shaking his head. I had not explained to her how to set the hook, what to do if a fish struck. Here was a lack of hope; I hadn't really believed that we might have a strike.

"Ah. We haven't talked about that, have we?"

"No."

"My fault. Did you see the fish hit the fly?"

"Yes." This was said with the implication that pretty much everyone with eyes could have seen that fish hit that fly, and if she just missed her chance, then I was in trouble. I became acutely aware of my daughter's talent for inflection.

"Okay, so next time, as soon as the fish hits, you just raise the rod. Straight up." I took the rod from her and showed her the motion. "Don't try to jerk the fish onto the bank. Just a solid set. Keep the line tight in your trigger finger or else it's all for nothing."

"So I just lift it up hard?"

"Not too hard, but yeah." I should have thought this through.

"Why didn't you tell me that?"

"Because I am a moron. Sorry. You got a moron for a dad."

She smiled at me and rolled her eyes in a way that said she agreed but forgave me. Then she cast again, not far enough. The fly drifted down and she picked up. I was coaching her aloud now.

"Okay, pick up. Back. Wait. Forward. Hard stop."

The fly looped over crudely but perfectly, landing a few feet above our previous strike. The fish came again. And just when it seemed that Paige wouldn't set the hook at all, she set the hook as if the fish were a whale. The fly burst from the water and caught in the willows behind us.

"A little late, kiddo. But a good set."

"I missed it."

"Not a problem. This fish will eat again."

I angled the line out of the tree and set her up again. Pick up. Back. Wait. Forward. Stop. The fly rolled over and plopped onto the surface several feet even farther upstream from our target. As soon as it landed an upstream fish hit it. And Paige struck. And the line went tight. Electric. Alive.

I was shouting something—a growl or a roar—I was filled with joy and hope and it exploded out of me in an unintelligible mess.

Paige cried: "WHAT DO I DO NOW?"

I managed to coach her enough to bring the fish into the bank. A ten-inch native cutthroat the color of wild fall leaves. A collage of tans and coppers, whites and oranges, black spots. It flopped in the shallow water among softball boulders and muddy sand. Paige held the bowed rod tight. We grinned at each other like two thieves.

"Do you want to release it?"

"Yeah." She grinned wider.

We knelt there at the place where land and water converge. I held the fish and removed the fly ("the thing with feathers"). Then my daughter put her hand into the stream and took the fish from me, keeping it wet, heeding my direction. The fish shivered and was ready to go. A volt of wild energy that was imprinting itself onto our memories.

"It's so pretty," she said. "It's so cool. Do I just let it swim?"

"Yeah, just open your hand."

She relaxed her grip, and the fish nuzzled free, waked the shallows, then disappeared back to wildness.

She looked at the stream with a mixture of awe and joy.

"You did it." I couldn't stop smiling.

"That was so cool."

A year later we drove to high country only to find the stream was a torrent of chocolate milk, unfishable due to heavy rains. When we got home after not even casting, my younger daughter, Ella, reminded me that I need to take her fishing. The day felt like a failure and a success, but I also got the impression that somewhere a clock was ticking.

Paige has begun riding horses. She downhill skis in the winter, she plays soccer in the summer, and she reads like a copy machine. Ella plays cello and piano and has begun working on a series of fantasy novels. I want them to do all of these things and more. I want them to drink up life like a trout in wild water. But I also want them *to want to fish* with me, and—at least for today—they do. Every summer we take a trip to small stream that is especially generous. It's something we all look forward to. It ties us to the land, and it ties us together.

I'm not sure they will ever feel the connection to wildness that I find in trout water. But I am okay with not knowing. What I learned that day on the river, the day of Paige's trout, was that trout water and public lands can connect me to my daughters the same way it can connect me to the elusive ideas of wildness and landscape. Trout streams are conduits for human relation. They connect me to my father and my brothers, to Packer—who is to me what Izaak Walton called "a Brother of the Angle" (1854, 3). And to my daughters and wife.

About halfway through his novella, Norman Maclean writes of a fishing trip in which his brother-in-law steals the beer Norman and his brother have sunk in the river to keep it cold: "What a beautiful world it was once. At least a river of it was. And it was almost mine and my family's and just a few others' who wouldn't steal beer" (2001, 56–57). This passage has always made me a little uncomfortable. I hate to imagine Maclean as someone who might want to take away river access based his evaluation of someone's moral character, though certainly beer stealing is a serious sin. But the more I think about public lands and waters, the more I like the passage. The river Maclean is referencing is the Big Blackfoot in Montana, a river that runs through public lands and offers public access. These rivers do belong to us (and just a few others—if we interpret broadly). And they certainly link families together. On that day when Paige caught her trout, that little cutthroat stream became our family river because it gave us a story in the same way the Macleans imbued the Big Blackfoot with the stories of fathers and sons. The only part of the passage I might change is the past tense. What a world it *is*, in large part because rivers like the Big Blackfoot are still public, still ours. The Blackfoot has even been nursed back to health after being poisoned by mining and development and nearly ruined. Its recovery can be linked directly with the success of Maclean's novel and the movie adaptation, directly to the Maclean family story. Rivers give us stories, and stories preserve rivers. Stories can protect rivers from those that would steal beer, and worse.

Now that they are interested in fly fishing, my job is to not lose my daughters' interest, and to not lose them by extension. Near the end of *A River Runs through It*, an aged Reverend Maclean goes fishing with his sons. He bemoans the fact that he cannot make his way down the steep bank and tells his boys he plans to fish downstream where the traverse is simpler. Before he walks off, Paul calls out to his father: "You'll get 'em." Maclean writes that his father was suddenly "confident in himself again" (2001, 84). Here the story has reversed, and the reverend—the man who taught his sons to cast on the lawn with a metronome, the man who preached that a fly cast was a way of connecting to the rhythms of God—relies on his sons to help him transcend his own human failings, to make him worthy of catching a trout.

If fly fishing and public lands are primarily an exercise in hope, then I hope for this. I hope for a day and for a geography where a word or smile from my knowing child lifts me above my own limitations, for a time and a place where they pull back the willows and lead me to a secret, wild creek in a public wilderness where a trout might rise with all the grace and beauty and hope that carries us all forward.

EPILOGUE

THE SHALLOW END OF
A NAMELESS LAKE

I was fourteen years old and twelve miles into the backcountry on the North Slope of the Uinta Mountains. My brother Justin and I were away from camp, hiking off trail, and looking for a lake. In the Uintas, you don't generally have to look far.

In this instance, the maps showed an unnamed lake one ridge over from the lake our Boy Scout troop was camped at, so it did not take us long to reach our destination, even though there was no real trail. We walked around the new lake, which felt miles from anywhere. I have never felt so isolated as I have fishing no-name, no-trail lakes a dozen miles from a trailhead.

Then, in a sudden rush of sound and wind and confusion, a small plane shattered the sky and the easy silence. It flew low over the granite peaks and dropped a payload of fingerling trout into the clear water.

I had never seen an aerial stocking, and I haven't seen one since. It was more than twenty years ago, but I remember the sound, the rushing whine of the engine that broke the wilderness calm, the heavy wind and metal of the plane as it roared into the granite bowl and blasted its way out as fast it came, the engine's volume chasing after.

We made our way around the lake to the shallow end and waded out to some boulders whose peaks triangled out of the water twenty feet from shore.

There—in the small waves sparkling around those boulders— were the casualties. Several dozen hatchery minnows hadn't survived the drop, floating in the shallows, telling us something about pine trees and stone, wild places, and man's attempts to tame anything so primal and impenetrable as a castle of gray stone peaks and the endless blue of mountain lakes.

Seeing those trout floating belly up in the shallows, I leaned close to listen, to hear something that goes on long and lasts into the dense star-filled black of a mountain night. Something that can't be spoken or made domestic. Something that exists in only a few wild places that haven't been bent to the service of commerce. Something that speaks quietly if it speaks at all. My brother and I waited, knowing that something important was happening.

I am still listening, sure there is something else to hear, leaning close and waiting.

REFERENCES

Colorado College. 2014. "Western States Survey." https://www
.coloradocollege.edu/dotAsset/d018420b-a728-%204dc5-9bd3
-157b6ec2beeb.pdf (page discontinued).

Cronon, William. 1996. "The Trouble with Wilderness: Or, Getting Back to the Wrong Nature." *Environmental History* 1, no.
1: 7–28.

Dickinson, Emily. 1964. *Final Harvest: Emily Dickinson's Poems.*
Edited by Thomas H. Johnson. Boston: Little, Brown.

Flores, Dan. 1999. *Horizontal Yellow: Nature and History in the
Near Southwest.* Albuquerque: University of New Mexico Press.

Gierach, John. 1999. *Standing in a River Waving a Stick.* New
York: Simon and Schuster.

Harrison, Jim. n.d. "Jim Harrison on the End of Nature." Accessed
April 26, 2018. *Men's Journal.* https://www.mensjournal.com
/features/jim-harrison-on-the-end-of-nature-w200869/.

Heaney, Seamus. 1998. *Open Ground: Select Poems 1966–1996.*
New York: Farrar, Straus and Giroux.

Hemingway, Ernest. 1987. *The Complete Short Stories of Ernest
Hemingway.* New York: Scribner.

Hotchner, A. E. 1966. *Papa Hemingway: A Personal Memoir.* New
York: Random House.

Hugo, Richard. 1984. *Making Certain It Goes On: The Collected
Poems of Richard Hugo.* New York: W. W. Norton.

Langston, Nancy. 2003. *Where Land and Water Meet: A Western
Landscape Transformed.* Seattle: University of Washington Press.

Leeson, Ted. 1994. *The Habit of Rivers: Reflections on Trout Streams
and Fly Fishing.* New York: Lyons Press.

Leopold, Aldo. 1989. *A Sand County Almanac*. New York: Oxford University Press.

Lyons, Nick. 1992. *Spring Creek*. New York: Atlantic Monthly Press.

Maclean, Norman. 2001. *A River Runs through It and Other Stories*. Chicago: University of Chicago Press.

McCarthy, Cormac. 2006. *The Road*. New York: Vintage Books.

Melville, Herman. 1967. *Moby-Dick*. New York: W. W. Norton.

Middleton, Harry. 1996. *The Earth Is Enough: Growing Up in a World of Flyfishing, Trout, and Old Men*. Boulder CO: Pruett.

Montana Department of Fish, Wildlife and Parks. n.d. "Stream Access in Montana: Rights and Responsibilities of Landowners and Recreationalists." Accessed April 26, 2018. http://fwp.mt .gov/fwpDoc.html?id=24929.

Posnanski, Joe. 2015. "My Favorite Year (1986)." *Joe*Blogs*. August 31. http://joeposnanski.com/my-favorite-year-redux/.

Putnam, N. F., Kenneth J. Lohmann, Emily M. Putman, Thomas P. Quinn, Peter Klimley, David L. G. Noakes. 2013. "Evidence for Geomagnetic Imprinting as a Homing Mechanism in Pacific Salmon." *Current Biology* 23, no. 4: 312–16.

Quammen, David. 2008. *Natural Acts: A Sidelong View of Science and Nature*. New York: W. W. Norton.

Snyder, Gary. 1990. *The Practice of the Wild*. Emeryville CA: Shoemaker and Hoard.

Stafford, William. 1978. *Writing the Australian Crawl: Views on the Writer's Vocation*. Ann Arbor: University of Michigan Press.

———. 1998. *The Way It Is: New and Selected Poems*. Minneapolis: Graywolf Press.

Stegner, Wallace. 1992. *Where the Bluebird Sings to the Lemonade Springs*. New York: Penguin Books.

———. 1997. *The Sound of Mountain Water*. New York: Penguin Books.

Thoreau, Henry David. 1995. *Walden*. London: Everyman.

———. 2001. *Collected Essays and Poems*. New York: Library of America.

U.S. Fish and Wildlife Service. 2014. "About Bull Trout." Last modified September 3, 2014. https://www.fws.gov/pacific /bulltrout/About.html.

Vincent, Carol H., Laura A. Hanson, and Carla N. Argueta. 2017. "Federal Land Ownership: Overview and Data." Congressional Research Service. Last modified March 3, 2017. https://fas.org /sgp/crs/misc/R42346.pdf.

Walton, Izaak. 1854. *The Complete Angler*. 2nd ed. London: Nathaniel Cook.

Wilbur, Richard. 1963. *The Poems of Richard Wilbur*. Boston: Mariner Books.

Wordsworth, William. 1994. *The Works of William Wordsworth*. Hertfordshire: Wordsworth Poetry Library.